Selected Papers of Allan Sproul

Edited by Lawrence S. Ritter

Federal Reserve Bank of New York

December 1980

Library of Congress Catalog Card Number 80-67915

Book Design: Joseph Penczak Design, Inc.

Printed in United States of America

ALLAN SPROUL

Table of Contents

Chapter 1

Allan Sproul, 1896-1978
"A Tower of Strength"

Chapter 2

Monetary Policy and Inflation

Chapter 3

Postwar Treasury-Federal Reserve Conflict and the Accord

Chapter 4

Human Judgment and Central Banking

Chapter 5

Deposit Interest Rate Ceilings

Chapter 6

Federal Reserve Structure and Monetary Policy

Chapter 7

Foreign Aid

Chapter 8

International Financial Problems

Portfolio of Photographs of Allan Sproul

Preface

The impetus for this volume to honor the memory of Allan Sproul came from Paul A. Volcker. As a young economist in the early fifties, Mr. Volcker worked at this Bank under Mr. Sproul. He remained in touch with him after he, in turn, became the Bank's President in 1975. Preparation of the volume, under Mr. Volcker's direction, was initiated several months before he was appointed Chairman of the Board of Governors of the Federal Reserve System.

Many people contributed to the preparation of this book. The Bank is particularly indebted to Lawrence S. Ritter, Professor of Finance at New York University, who made the final selection of the material to be included, edited where necessary, and arranged the papers. He wrote the introductory biographical sketch of Mr. Sproul and the chapter introductions.

In the process of gathering information for the introductory biography, Professor Ritter was generously assisted by several people whose help was invaluable. They include Charles A. Coombs, Robert V. Roosa, Robert G. Rouse, William F. Treiber, and Thomas O. Waage, all of whom had been colleagues of Mr. Sproul at this Bank; Richard P. Cooley, Chairman of the Board, Wells Fargo Bank; Murray J. Rossant, Director, The Twentieth Century Fund; and last, but by no means least, Mary C. Regan, Mr. Sproul's secretary at the Federal Reserve Bank of New York for twenty-five years.

Carl W. Backlund, Chief, Central Records and Archives Division of this Bank, undertook the initial sifting and winnowing of the large volume of Mr. Sproul's papers—including his speeches, articles, Congressional testimony, internal memoranda, and letters. Stephen V.O. Clarke, Research Officer and Senior Economist, then reduced this material to manageable proportions, organized it in terms of subject matter, and made a preliminary selection of papers for inclusion in the book.

To all of them, we owe a deep debt of gratitude.

Anthony M. Solomon
President

December 1980

Foreword

Allan Sproul was the third chief executive officer of the Federal Reserve Bank of New York, having been its President from January 1941 until he retired in June 1956. He came to this Bank as Secretary in 1930, after serving during the twenties at the Federal Reserve Bank of San Francisco.

His interest in public policy and central banking was lifelong. Those who knew him were invariably impressed with the breadth of his vision combined with technical competence, the strength of his convictions combined with a grace and temperance in intellectual combat, the sense of dignity and position combined with a warmth of personal friendship. During his presidency of the "New York Fed", he stimulated a whole generation of Federal Reserve officials to find their careers in central banking and related professions, fostering monetary stability in this country and international economic cooperation. Throughout his "retirement", he continued to support those causes, consulting with those from Presidents on down who sought his judgment.

The volume of his writings—published and unpublished—bears testimony to the scope of his interests and the quality of his thought. A representative selection from these writings is of more than historical interest, and a fitting memorial for a great central banker.

Paul A. Volcker

December 1980

Chapter 1

Allan Sproul
1896-1978
"A Tower of Strength"

Allan Sproul, president of the Federal Reserve Bank of New York from 1941 to 1956 and one of history's most talented central bankers, died in California on April 9, 1978, at the age of eighty-two. His passing was widely mourned, even though he had been in semiretirement for over two decades, for few who had come in contact with him ever forgot him.

He made an imposing first impression: in his prime a ruggedly built 200-pound bear of a man, somewhat under six feet tall, with a disarming smile and a vigorous tone of voice. "He looked as solid", someone once said, "as the Federal Reserve Bank itself."

However, it was his intellectual vitality that made a more lasting impression on those who got to know him for any length of time. He had a finely honed sense of humor and an almost instinctive feel for the English language—an uncanny ability to turn a phrase with style and grace. These qualities, combined with a deep devotion to what might be called old-fashioned ideals and principles, including the work ethic, made him a formidable adversary. A voracious reader, especially of classical literature, history, and biography, he was constantly bringing his learning to bear on current policymaking problems, constantly searching for general principles that might help explain current developments by putting them in perspective against the broad sweep of history.

Nor did this change in the twenty-two years following his premature retirement from the Federal Reserve Bank of New York in 1956, at the age of sixty. For central banking was more than a vocation to him—it was a passion, and it remained so until the very day of his death.

The pride he took in his profession, which he was usually too reserved to show, was inadvertently revealed during Hearings of the Senate Committee on Banking and Currency in 1945. Senator Tobey, intending to be complimentary, said at one point: "You are approaching this thing as a banker, as you should, backed by all the conservatism and good judgment that you have acquired by years of experience."

But Sproul was more irritated than flattered. "I appear here not as a banker," he responded, "but as a central banker. There is quite a distinction. I have no years of conservatism behind me. I have years of trying to improve and develop and liberalize the functioning of the domestic and international banking machinery."[1]

Allan Sproul was born in San Francisco on March 9, 1896, the second son of Robert and Sarah Elizabeth Sproul. His father had been born in Scotland and emigrated in the 1880s to California, where he found employment as a freight auditor for the Southern Pacific Railroad. His older brother, Robert Gordon, born in 1891, rose to the presidency of the University of California, a position he held from 1930 until his retirement in 1958. Like his brother, Allan always considered himself a Californian, despite the quarter century he spent in the New York financial community. New York was challenging and exciting, but it was never home.

Allan's youth and early adulthood were spent almost entirely in the San Francisco Bay Area. He went to elementary school first in San Francisco and later in Berkeley, after the family moved across the Bay, and in due course attended high school there and then the University of California at Berkeley. His college career was interrupted by America's entrance into World War I. He promptly enlisted in the Army Air Force and excitedly learned to fly rickety fighter planes at Mather Field near Sacramento—a bare fourteen years after the Wright Brothers' first flight at Kitty Hawk in 1903.

"Aviation used to have a chivalrous aspect," he recalled years later. "We flew by feel and touch, enjoying the rush of wind in our faces. Now I look at the instrument panels in airplanes and wonder how we ever did it."[2]

[1] United States Senate Committee on Banking and Currency, *Hearings on Bretton Woods Agreements Act* (June 21, 1945), p. 310.
[2] *The Fed*, Federal Reserve Bank of New York (September 28, 1955), pp. 7-8.

2

He arrived in England with his squadron late in 1918, but hostilities ended before he flew any combat missions. The war over, he returned to the University of California and graduated in 1919 with a degree in agriculture. He went to work briefly with the California Packing Company, which dealt in farm produce, and then as an agricultural adviser for two small banks in Southern California. In 1920, however, he accepted a position as head of the research department at the Federal Reserve Bank of San Francisco, thereby beginning a career in the Federal Reserve System that would last for thirty-six years.

Given his background, how did he get such a job in the first place? Fortunately, Sproul's own recollections of his start in the Federal Reserve System have been preserved in the form of a transcript of an after-dinner talk he gave in San Francisco in 1976, shortly after his eightieth birthday:[3]

> This will not be one of my offbeat reports on the elusive aspects of domestic monetary and fiscal policies, nor on the more intricate aspects of the international monetary system. I thought a personal memoir on the triumph of serendipity (discovering by chance things one has not sought) over rational determination in finding and following a career would be more in keeping with the occasion.
>
> About fifty-six years ago, I entered the fringe of banking. I had recently been graduated from the College of Agriculture at the University of California at Berkeley, clutching a B.S. degree in pomology, which is fruit growing for those of you whose Latin is a little rusty. I had learned one thing, at least, in earning my degree. I was not cut out to be a farmer.
>
> Fortunately, as things turned out, a friend of mine had recently become assistant to the chairman of the fledgling Federal Reserve Bank of San Francisco. He allowed himself to be deceived into thinking I might know something about banking because I was temporarily masquerading as a bank agriculturalist at two small banks in Southern California, among the orange and lemon groves and walnut orchards. He lured me away from that rural scene with the offer of a

---

[3] Talk at Wells Fargo Bank Directors Dinner, April 19, 1976.

job as head of the Division of Analysis and Research at the Reserve Bank. It really didn't matter to him, nor to me, that I knew little about banking and nothing about central banking.

In fact, I did not know what a central bank was, which is not so strange as it might now seem. No one else hereabouts knew much about central banking then, and even now not many people know what it is all about. All that I really had to do, to get started, was to develop a nascent facility for assembling facts and figures, and for presenting them to my superiors in readable fashion and, through them, to the Federal Reserve Board at Washington, concerning agricultural, business, and credit conditions in the seven Western states which then comprised the Twelfth Federal Reserve District. Now, with greater sophistication and with the workings of Parkinson's Law, squadrons of people and phalanxes of computers do the same thing.

Later, I became the assistant to the chairman and Secretary of the Bank, which enabled me to hire the equivalent of a couple of present-day M.B.A.s to do the analysis and research, while I devoted myself to learning how policy is made, and other loftier pursuits. This included making the acquaintance of some notable San Franciscans who were directors of the Bank.

My most rewarding contact, however, was with my immediate boss, John Perrin, the chairman of the board, which was then a full-time job. He was a testy old gentleman about ten years younger than I am now, who had come out of retirement to help get the Reserve System started. He had a real interest in developing the art of central banking, and he demanded that I become a serious student of the occult calling. He also demanded that I pay scrupulous attention to the niceties of the English language. It was not always an easy relationship, but it was a rewarding one.

Sproul's position as Secretary of the San Francisco Bank, which he assumed in 1924, entailed occasional cross-country trips to Washington for monetary policy conferences. At those meetings his abilities attracted the attention of Benjamin Strong, head of the Federal Reserve Bank of New York, and George L. Harrison, Strong's deputy. Early in 1928, Harrison, on Strong's behalf, discreetly sounded out the young Californian: would he be interested in transferring to the Federal Reserve Bank of New York?

Although Sproul was intrigued by the possibility of working in the nation's financial center, he was reluctant to leave the West Coast. In 1921 he had married Marion Bogle. They had met as classmates at the University of California, and by 1929 they had three sons—Allan, Jr., Gordon, and David—and were happy in their Bay Area home. Late in 1928 Benjamin Strong died but Harrison, his successor as head of the New York Bank, continued to renew the invitation.

With Sproul hesitant and Harrison persistent, negotiations dragged on for over a year. Finally, in 1930, with the stock market in disarray and the economy sliding downhill, the opportunity to get into the thick of things became too tempting to turn down any longer: the 33-year-old Sproul accepted Harrison's offer and brought his family east.

The thirties were years of desperation and frustration for most Americans, but for Allan Sproul they were years of development and growth. He joined the New York Bank on March 1, 1930, spent his first few years as Secretary, the same position he had held at the San Francisco Bank, and was assigned to the foreign department. In the latter role he began to get deeply involved for the first time in international monetary affairs, an area that soon fascinated him and was to remain a major interest throughout his life. The old international financial order was collapsing, and repeated efforts to prop it up were proving fruitless. Along with Harrison, Sproul participated in international monetary conferences and came to know many of his counterparts abroad, including the fabled Montagu Norman, long-time head of the Bank of England.

He also came to know Professor John H. Williams of Harvard University, a man whose advice and counsel he grew to value immensely. Williams became an officer of the Federal Reserve Bank of New York in the early thirties, and continued as such for over three decades, all the while retaining his professorship at Harvard. Nine years Sproul's senior, Williams was a world-renowned authority on international finance, combining theoretical expertise with a bent for the practicalities of the everyday world. There developed between them a mutual respect and fondness that ripened with the years. At first with Williams as teacher and Sproul as pupil, and later as equals, the two conducted a continual dialogue on international finance—in corridors, over lunch, after business hours—that lasted for more than twenty years.

In 1934 Sproul became Harrison's assistant, a newly created position; what Harrison had been to Strong, Sproul now became to Harrison. In 1936 he was promoted again, this time to first vice president. In September 1938, however, W. Randolph Burgess accepted an offer to become vice chairman of the National City Bank of New York and resigned as manager of the System Open Market Account, a position in which he had been responsible for conducting open market operations on behalf of the entire Federal Reserve System under the direction of the Federal Open Market Committee. Sproul was rushed into the gap and, while remaining first vice president, spent the next fifteen months conducting the Federal Reserve's open market operations—an experience that, although he could hardly know it at the time, would stand him in good stead not too many years later.

Shortly thereafter, in 1940, George Harrison decided to call it a day. With the enactment of the Banking Act of 1935, which Harrison had not favored, the balance of power in the Federal Reserve began shifting from the nation's financial capital to its political capital. The New York Bank no longer dominated the System, as it had in the heyday of Benjamin Strong, and Harrison chafed under what he considered undue interference from Washington. In addition, he had never gotten along with the peppery Marriner Eccles, since 1934 chairman of the Board of Governors in Washington and principal architect of the Banking Act of 1935. Friction between them had only increased with the passage of time. Thus after twelve years at the helm George Harrison resigned in 1940, at the age of fifty-three, to become president of the New York Life Insurance Company. The man chosen to replace him was the man he himself had persuaded to leave California a decade earlier.

On January 1, 1941, Allan Sproul became the third president of the Federal Reserve Bank of New York and shortly thereafter vice chairman of the Federal Open Market Committee, the System's main policymaking body.

Sproul had hardly assumed his new positions before he became immersed in the complexities of war finance. Early in 1942 the Federal Reserve, after consultation with the Treasury, announced that it would assure ample funds for the war effort by maintaining a fixed pattern of interest rates on Government securities for the duration—ranging from 3/8 percent on three-month Treasury bills to 7/8 percent on one-year certificates, through about 2 percent on ten-year bonds, and on out to 2½ percent on the longest marketable issues. The purpose of maintaining a fixed pattern of rates was to make clear to potential buyers that they had nothing to gain by postponing purchases of Government securities, since none would be issued later at higher yields. The yield pattern would be maintained, of course, by the Federal Reserve itself acting as a residual buyer, thereby keeping securities prices from falling and interest rates from rising.

Both Eccles and Sproul preferred higher rates at the short end than 3/8 percent and 7/8 percent, feeling that the spread between short and long rates was too great. Nevertheless, with the country at war, the System, under pressure from Secretary of the Treasury Henry Morgenthau, Jr., had no choice but to agree to the details of the program. As Eccles and Sproul had warned, however, the excessive spread resulted in most of the short-term securities eventually being dumped on the Federal Reserve, while banks and others held the higher yielding long-term issues instead. Looking back, several years later, Sproul wrote:[4]

> If mistakes were made in this period, as they were, the principal one was the too rigid maintenance of the pattern of rates and unwillingness to let the short rate fluctuate (rise) somewhat. A modest rise in short-term rates could have further mobilized unused reserves in banks outside the money centers and in the hands of nonbank investors; would have taken account of the fact that as the war progressed the amount of idle funds declined, demands grew, and stability of long-term rates became accepted; would have narrowed the spread between short and long rates and the consequent riding of the pattern; and might have preserved a slight but healthy degree of unpredictability in the short and intermediate rate area. Since some movement of short rates could probably have taken place without much, if any, overall increase in cost to the Treasury and without disturbing the maintenance of long rates, it was and is difficult to justify dogged adherence to a "fixed" rate pattern, but that was the final decision of the war period.

[4] Allan Sproul, "Changing Concepts of Central Banking", in *Money, Trade, and Economic Growth,* Essays in Honor of John Henry Williams (New York: Macmillan, 1951), pp. 304-5.

In general, the war was financed more by the creation of new money than Eccles or Sproul thought advisable or necessary, resulting in the buildup of an inflationary potential that was to cause grave problems after the cessation of hostilities. In his 1951 autobiography, Eccles recalled that Sproul was "particularly helpful and constructive" in devising less inflationary methods of war finance—most of which, unfortunately, were not adopted by the Treasury.

"We sometimes disagreed over policy matters," Eccles said of Sproul, "but our differences were never marked by personal acrimony. Sproul was and is first and foremost a representative of the public interest. He has been and is a tower of strength in the Reserve System."[5]

As the war gradually tilted in the Allies' favor, Sproul began to devote more of his attention to the numerous plans that were in the air for postwar domestic and international economic reform. For the most part, he was against them. In 1945 he wrote to the Senate Banking and Currency Committee opposing the Full Employment Act, expressing concern with respect to excessive Government interference in the economy: "Just as there seems to be a limit of tolerance of the woes and evils of alternate boom and depression, there is probably also a limit of tolerance of Government intervention in what we call private enterprise, if it is to remain private enterprise."[6]

He was also skeptical about the proposed International Monetary Fund (IMF), believing it to be premature and self-defeating, and caused somewhat of a stir when alone among Federal Reserve officials he testified in that vein before the Congress in 1945. But he endorsed its companion International Bank for Reconstruction and Development (the World Bank), viewing it as a more appropriate vehicle for easing the severe dislocations in the immediate postwar period.

Something like the IMF, he suggested, would be better left until a postwar transition period had enabled the world economy to get on its feet again, at which time exchange rates could be established on a more realistic basis. Even then, he felt, the international financial system would be better served by agreements among the principal trading and financial nations, with the smaller countries adapting to those agreements, rather than in a forum that perpetuated the illusion that all nations are equal insofar as international commerce is concerned. To him, the "democratic" organizational structure of the IMF all but

---

[5] Marriner Eccles, *Beckoning Frontiers* (New York: Knopf, 1951), pp. 363-64.

[6] United States Senate Committee on Banking and Currency, *Hearings on Full Employment Act of 1945*, p. 1219.

guaranteed "a diffusion of authority and responsibility which is almost fatal".[7]

In fact, the IMF turned out to be far more successful than Sproul had expected, as he later admitted, and he eventually became an advocate of many of its tenets—although never of its organizational structure. One of the features of the IMF that particularly appealed to him was the relative stability of exchange rates that it fostered. (His earlier opposition was partly because he thought its charter encouraged excessive rate flexibility.) Floating exchange rates, championed by most academic economists, left him unimpressed. He viewed floating rates as an impediment to the free flow of international commerce and a spurious solution to the underlying domestic problems they were supposed to resolve; by helping nations postpone the hard decisions they often had to make to live within their means, floating rates frequently made matters all the worse.

Indeed, he was frequently at odds with the conventional wisdom of economists, and over the years found himself in what can only be described as a love-hate relationship with economic theory. He admired and respected economic analysis that was firmly grounded in reality, and for that reason built up the research department of the Federal Reserve Bank of New York to the point where its prestige rivaled that of the economics departments of the top universities. It was by far his favorite department in the Bank, the one where he felt most at home. It was not unusual for him, after reading a memorandum prepared by an economist in the research department, to amble down to the surprised memo-writer's office for a chat about the issues involved.

Years later, speaking before the American Economic Association and the American Finance Association in 1966, he recalled those days:[8]

> Paul Samuelson once said that the economists of the Federal Reserve System had only one idea, which he didn't think was enough, although he said they were better than the economists of the Bank of England who had only half an idea. That is funny but not factual. At the Federal Reserve Bank of New York we were drawing on some of the best economic brains coming out of Harvard—and other institutions of higher learning—before the government at

[7] Talk at Board of Directors meeting, Wells Fargo Bank, August 16, 1977.

[8] Allan Sproul, "Coordination of Economic Policy", *Journal of Finance* (May 1967), pp. 137-38.

Washington fully waked up to the possibilities of such recruitment. The "Age of the Economist", which Walter Heller hailed in his Godkin lectures at Harvard this spring, came early to the New York Reserve Bank. Ideas flowed freely, balances governing problems of choice were struck by economists "in terms a decision maker could sink his teeth into", and I was a beneficiary of this sort of fruitful collaboration for many years. I miss it.

At the same time, he was impatient, even disdainful, of idealized abstractions, no matter how finely spun, that he felt neglected the nuances and complexities of the real world. The intimate familiarity he had developed with the foreign exchange markets when he was in the foreign department in the early thirties, and with the domestic money and capital markets when he managed the Federal Reserve's open market operations, left their mark in the form of a lasting understanding of and respect for the many ways financial markets function and evolve. As a result of these experiences, he grew increasingly restive with much of formal economics, feeling that it ignored or misconstrued market realities and was therefore a naive (and often misleading) guide to public policy.

Once, writing from retirement in California to a young former colleague still at the New York Federal Reserve Bank, he expressed that skepticism in his typical pungent fashion. Referring to a mutual acquaintance who had put forth certain proposals with respect to monetary policy, he wrote:[9]

> . . .he has a strong tendency toward cosmic thinking and metaphysical roundabouts. Beneath all of the wordy embroidery he is really distrustful of the money market and the people who operate it. . . .This is a legacy, perhaps, of a fundamentalist religious slant as bent and twisted by the University of Chicago, but it is also a consequence of his having had no experience in a money market. Whatever your own future may be, I think you can be thankful that, at one stage, you had to rub your nose in the market.

[9] Letter from Sproul to Robert V. Roosa, April 27, 1959.

World War II had hardly ended before Allan Sproul faced a difficult decision. In 1946 he was offered the presidency of the World Bank, and he and Marion spent weeks agonizing over whether or not he should accept it. As usual, he wrote down all the arguments, pro and con, on a legal-sized yellow pad before coming to a final decision. Long ago, he had found that the best way to crystallize his thoughts was on paper, so that whenever he faced a complex or difficult problem, professional or personal, he would sit at his desk and methodically write down the issues, point by point, before making up his mind.

Finally, he decided to remain at the Federal Reserve Bank. His notes mention, among other things: "Approaching critical opportunity in life of FR System and would like to play out that string." Also: "The World Bank's operations may well be more political (in broad sense) than economic. I do not like and am not too good at the sort of politico-economics and politico-administration which seems inevitable."[10]

He could not have been more correct in his assessment that the Federal Reserve indeed faced a critical juncture in its history, a crossroads that was to have major implications for its future role in the economy. But little did he realize how "political" the entire matter would become—had he known, he might well have chosen the World Bank!

With the war over, many in the Federal Reserve felt the time had come to begin terminating the interest rate pegs that had been maintained since 1942. By standing ready to buy securities at any and all times solely to keep their prices from falling and yields from rising—buying at the market's initiative rather than its own—the central bank had lost control over bank reserves and the money supply. It had become, in Marriner Eccles' famous words, "an engine of inflation".

The Treasury, however, saw things in a different light: tighter money and higher interest rates would raise the cost of servicing a swollen Federal debt and might possibly precipitate another depression. Why not, therefore, continue to keep money ample and interest rates low?

It was not until mid-1947 that the Federal Reserve was able to secure Treasury permission to remove the 3/8 percent peg on Treasury bills, and then the 7/8 percent peg on certificates. The 2½ percent long rate remained sacrosanct, even though a Congressional subcommittee chaired by Senator Douglas, after exploring the controversy, recommended in January 1950 that the Federal Reserve, not the Treasury, should be responsible for and determine monetary policy.

[10] Sproul handwritten notes, "Considerations Involved in Offer of Presidency of World Bank", dated December 22, 1946, Federal Reserve Bank of New York.

But the Douglas Committee's recommendations only heated up the dispute. Unconvinced, Secretary of the Treasury John W. Snyder continued to insist on having the final say in monetary matters, a final say that effectively aborted anti-inflationary actions by the central bank.

The controversy came to a head on Wednesday, January 31, 1951, when President Truman asked the members of the Federal Open Market Committee (of which Sproul was vice chairman) to meet with him at the White House. On Thursday and Friday the press was informed through White House and Treasury sources that at Wednesday's White House meeting the Federal Reserve had agreed to the President's request to support Government securities prices and to maintain stable interest rates. This was at variance with the Open Market Committee's impression of what had occurred, and to set the record straight Marriner Eccles, over the weekend and on his own initiative, hastily released to the press the Federal Reserve's memorandum of what had transpired.

Eccles clearly exceeded his authority in taking it upon himself to release the Federal Reserve's version of the White House meeting. He was still a member of the Board of Governors and of the Open Market Committee, but no longer chairman (having been relieved of that position in 1948 by President Truman and replaced by Thomas B. McCabe). Normal procedure would have been to wait until the weekend had passed and leave the decision to Chairman McCabe and the full Board. What followed immediately thereafter was related by Eccles in his autobiography:[11]

> By Monday morning the fat was in the fire. Rather than wait for the scheduled meeting on February 13, McCabe called the Open Market Committee to meet on the next day, Tuesday, February 6. The purpose was to consider what should be done in view of the weekend development. With the exception of Allan Sproul, no one at the meeting either approved or criticized my action in releasing the memorandum. Sproul expressed the view that what goes on at a Presidential conference should not be disclosed until the President gives it out, but when the President does that he should give an accurate report of what has happened. It was

[11] Eccles, *op. cit.*, p. 497.

the Board's memorandum that accurately represented what was actually said and the spirit in which it was said. For this reason, Sproul continued, he was glad I had taken individual action in releasing the memorandum; it temporarily retrieved our place in the financial community and with the public.

In my reply I expressed regret that the situation had developed to the point where releasing a confidential document seemed absolutely essential. I purposely avoided telling anybody what I was going to do because I did not want to involve anyone else in any way.

At Sproul's suggestion, the Open Market Committee thereupon agreed that letters would be drafted to President Truman and Secretary of the Treasury Snyder to get the issue back on an official basis. Later in the week McCabe and Sproul, as chairman and vice chairman of the Open Market Committee, met with leaders of the Senate Banking and Currency Committee and of the Joint Economic Committee, all of whom advised, in Sproul's words, "that it was no time for feuding and no time for a Congressional hearing, but a time for the Treasury and the Federal Reserve to try again to compose their differences".[12]

Several weeks of difficult negotiations followed, including another meeting of McCabe and Sproul with the President on February 26. However, on March 4, 1951, the Treasury-Federal Reserve "Accord" was finally announced. The effect of the agreement was to restore the independence of the Federal Reserve to pursue flexible monetary policies for the first time since 1942. Purchases of short-term securities were promptly discontinued and, although the Federal Reserve continued to buy longer issues for a brief period, they were bought at gradually declining prices (gradually rising yields) and in a few months ceased altogether. The pegged 2½ percent long rate had finally passed into history.

But, if Allan Sproul thought that the Accord meant that his unwilling involvement in "politico-administration" was over, and that the painful stomach ulcers he had acquired would now subside in a period of goodwill and tranquillity, he was sadly mistaken.

[12] Allan Sproul, "The 'Accord'—A Landmark in the First Fifty Years of the Federal Reserve System", *Monthly Review* of the Federal Reserve Bank of New York (November 1964), p. 231.

Shortly after the Accord, Thomas McCabe resigned as chairman of the Board of Governors and was replaced by William McChesney Martin, who until then had been assistant secretary of the Treasury. In July 1951 Marriner Eccles also resigned, after more than sixteen years on the Board, to return home to Utah. As the Open Market Committee began to grow familiar with conducting open market operations freely once again, it appointed an Ad Hoc Subcommittee to explore the functioning of the Government securities market and to examine its effectiveness as a conduit for central bank policies.

The Ad Hoc Subcommittee submitted its report late in 1952. Its principal findings were that the Government securities market lacked sufficient "depth, breadth, and resiliency" to be an effective transmission mechanism for the implementation of monetary policy and that these characteristics should be improved and strengthened. To accomplish those ends, it recommended that henceforth the Federal Reserve confine its open market operations strictly to Treasury bills, except to correct disorderly market conditions.

In September 1953, after a bitter nine-month battle within the Open Market Committee, the "bills only" policy was duly adopted as operating procedure for the conduct of open market operations. The vote was nine to two, with Allan Sproul leading the opposition.

The majority position was that the constant threat of Federal Reserve open market intervention throughout the maturity structure introduced a capricious element that prevented the Government securities market from functioning as well as it might. A policy of minimum intervention—confining open market operations to Treasury bills—would permit the market to grow and develop and thereby enable it to reflect more accurately underlying supply and demand forces. "Bills only" would not hamper the effectiveness of monetary policy, because an initial change in short-term yields would soon spread over the entire maturity range through the market's own arbitrage. In fact, it would enhance the effectiveness of monetary policy, because the greater the "depth, breadth, and resiliency" of the market the more promptly changes in yields at the short end would spread throughout the maturity structure.

Sproul argued vehemently against this position on the grounds that with experience the market would grow and develop on its own, learning by itself how best to adapt to open market operations in all areas. Confining operations to Treasury bills could on occasion reduce the effectiveness of monetary policy because changes in short-term yields do not always spread to other sectors speedily enough. When intermediate and longer yields respond sluggishly, some direct operations in longer issues may be necessary to start them moving or to keep them moving once they have started.

Other issues complicated the debate and gave it an emotional undertow that perhaps dragged the leading participants further than they had originally intended. One was the traditional suspicion between Washington and New York, a tug-of-war that had considerable precedent in Federal Reserve history. The very appointment of the Ad Hoc Subcommittee, in Sproul's words, "had been conceived by members of the staff of the Board of Governors (and of the Open Market Committee) who not only were interested in the operation of the Government securities market as a channel through which to reach and regulate the reserve position of the member banks, but who also were dissatisfied with the performance of the management of the System Open Market Account at the Federal Reserve Bank of New York and with the power distribution involved in the linkage between policymaking by the Federal Open Market Committee at Washington and the execution of policy by the New York Bank".[13]

As if that were not enough, a disagreement that began over practice soon took on the mantle of principle for both sides. The majority spokesman, William McChesney Martin, viewed minimum intervention ("bills only") as the philosophical opposite of maximum intervention (outright pegging of Government securities prices and interest rates, as had been the practice prior to the Accord). If maximum intervention was bad central banking, then minimum intervention must be good central banking. What better way to prove that the Federal Reserve was no longer in the business of determining, fixing, or supporting intermediate and long rates than total abstention from those sectors?

The implication, which Sproul resented, was that anyone who opposed "bills only" was somehow philosophically in league with the proponents of pegging and support operations. It was an implication he found particularly odious, since he had been in the forefront of the Federal Reserve's fight with the Treasury over that very matter. Indeed, he found it ironic that he had to defend himself on this issue against Martin, who as assistant secretary of the Treasury at the time had been

---

[13] Allan Sproul, "Policy Norms and Central Banking", *Men, Money, and Policy,* Essays in Honor of Karl R. Bopp (Federal Reserve Bank of Philadelphia, 1970), pp. 72-73.

one of the Treasury's chief representatives in the negotiations leading up to the Accord.

For Sproul also, the controversy took on broader significance. He felt that to replace the rigidity of maintaining a pattern of rates with the rigidity of "bills only" was only to move from one straitjacket to another. Central banking cannot be reduced, he said, "to an unchanging formula with 'rules of the game' which can be published, say, like the rules of baseball".[14]

> There are no wholly "free" money and capital markets so long as a central bank exists and does its job under modern conditions. There must be private markets—unpegged markets—the pulses of which can be taken in determining central bank policy, but the actions of the central bank, no matter how or in what section of the market they take place, will always be a major influence on the private market and a major factor in its expectations. The search by a central bank for some mechanical guide to automatic action, for some norm of behavior, in order to avoid the risks of fallible human judgments, ends up as a form of self-deception.
>
> The central bank should exert its influence on the cost and availability of capital and credit openly and directly, as circumstances may require, in whatever areas of the market it can reach. To do less is to abdicate a responsibility and to forfeit a power which has been granted for public use.[15]

The continual struggle was getting to him. His ulcers had become so bad that it would take a week of milk and bland foods following the tension of every Open Market Committee meeting before he began to feel well again. In December 1954 he testified head-on against Chairman Martin on the subject of "bills only", before a subcommittee of the Joint Economic Committee—a painful experience for a long-time organization man who respected and believed in the hierarchical structure of the Federal Reserve System. He was getting more public attention then he sought or felt comfortable with.

[14] Allan Sproul, "The Federal Reserve System—Working Partner of the National Banking System for Half a Century", *Banking and Monetary Studies* (Irwin, 1963), p. 66.

[15] Allan Sproul, *Statement Submitted to the Royal Commission on Banking and Finance,* Ottowa, Canada, September 27, 1962, pp. 22-23.

Sometime in 1955 he began for the first time to think seriously about possibly leaving the Federal Reserve System. It had been his home for thirty-five years, but things were no longer the same. Was the role he found himself playing helpful or harmful to the System's objectives? Perhaps both he and the System would be better off if they parted? It took him a year to make up his mind. When he finally did, in late April 1956, he called his senior colleagues into his office, one by one, and told them of his decision. None had had any prior inkling of what had been going through his mind. He then issued the following statement:[16]

It is with real regret that I have resigned my post as president of the Federal Reserve Bank of New York. I have done so only because Mrs. Sproul and I feel that personal needs and wishes can now take precedence over public duties.

I have spent thirty-six years in the Federal Reserve System, all but ten of them in New York. For the last fifteen years and a few months I have served as head of the New York Federal Reserve Bank and as vice chairman of the Federal Open Market Committee. I am grateful to the directors of the Bank and to my associates on the Committee for having given me the opportunity to serve in these important posts.

The proper functioning of the Federal Reserve System is of enormous importance, not only to our economy but to the whole fabric of our community life; the broadly based structure of the System is an outstanding accomplishment of our democratic and federal government. I have always been proud that I have been able to play a part in the formulation and execution of the System's policies during critical years of war and peace. I expect to continue to be one of the System's firmest friends after I sever my formal connection with it.

I have no immediate plans for the future beyond returning to California and reestablishing my home there, with the hope that the opportunities for enjoying the pleasures of family life will be greater than they have been in recent years.

[16] Press Statement, Federal Reserve Bank of New York, April 30, 1956.

His resignation was effective June 30, 1956, and shortly thereafter he and Marion drove cross-country to the West Coast. Afterward, he wrote back to a friend describing the exultation they both felt when they reached their home state. They made sure to note the exact time when they crossed the border from Nevada into California!

The Sprouls settled in Kentfield, a small community in Marin County, some twenty miles northwest of San Francisco. Now he had time to rest, to unwind, to reflect, and both of them had a chance to enjoy each other's company once again.

But retirement from the Bank, at the age of sixty, did not mean inactivity. After a while he became associated with the American Trust Company—and later with the Wells Fargo Bank, after the two institutions merged in 1960—first as a director and then as a consultant. As part of that association, he began making regular monthly talks at directors' meetings on current monetary and fiscal policies, international financial affairs, and related subjects. He prepared for these as painstakingly as he had formerly prepared for Open Market Committee meetings, researching meticulously and writing out everything beforehand. (He never spoke to any group extemporaneously, if he could avoid it.) These talks were so enthusiastically received that he continued to deliver them regularly until a couple of months before he died.

With some leisure time at his disposal for a change, he also permitted himself the luxury of fully gratifying his desire to write. Always a prolific letter writer, he now indulged himself, and regularly at length communicated his views on current economic developments to the host of friends and former colleagues he had left behind on the East Coast. Typically, his letters were carefully thought through and composed with a flair for expression that flowed without seeming effort. In addition, he wrote a number of articles on various aspects of central banking. However, to the very end he steadfastly refused all efforts to get him to write his memoirs.

Nor did his career in public service come to an end. Throughout the 1960s he served, from time to time, in an advisory capacity to various governmental bodies and private public-interest organizations, such as the Committee for Economic Development and the Twentieth Century Fund. In early 1960 he traveled to India and Pakistan, as a member of a three-man commission appointed by the World Bank, to examine the role of foreign aid in the economic development of those countries.

18

And in early 1961 he chaired a three-man committee, named by then President-elect Kennedy, charged with advising the new administration on measures to strengthen both the domestic economy and this country's balance-of-payments position. The Committee's report, transmitted to President-elect Kennedy on January 18, 1961, was written jointly by all three members (Roy Blough, Paul McCracken, and Sproul), but it was not difficult to identify the one responsible for a prominent section that recommended more flexible monetary policies in terms of the range of open market operations.

The following month, on February 20, 1961, the Open Market Committee suddenly announced that it was discarding "bills only" because of a conflict between domestic objectives and balance-of-payments goals. Confronted by a recession and a payments deficit, the Federal Reserve began to conduct open market operations throughout the maturity structure, in an attempt to lower long-term rates (to stimulate domestic business expansion) while simultaneously raising short-term yields (to prevent an outflow of money market funds abroad).

The abandonment of "bills only" in February 1961 turned out to be a permanent change in the conduct of monetary policy. At the time, however, it was not clear whether the change was permanent or temporary. In response to one of many congratulatory messages, Sproul replied with a brief note: "As you surmised, I am delighted that time and circumstance have combined to demonstrate that it is folly to tie your hands with an inflexible rule. Although the boys are still talking about a return to chastity when the present combination of domestic recession and a balance-of-payments deficit is no longer with us, it will be hard to regain a state of virginity. I hope the idea will be allowed a quiet burial."[17]

As the 1960s unfolded, he became increasingly concerned about America's involvement in Vietnam. In 1966 he wrote to a friend: "I am glad that you have attained a certain status among the Administration's policymakers as an 'objectionable character'—*i.e.*, one who does not accept the party line without question. With respect to the domestic economic situation—and the Vietnam war—I think they have backed into policies which they now do not know how to change, and have descended to calling those who disagree uncomplimentary names."[18]

[17] Letter from Sproul to James Coggeshall, Jr., March 5, 1961.
[18] Letter from Sproul to Murray J. Rossant, February 11, 1966.

As the war heated up, so did his feelings. "I am so much against our involvement on the Asian mainland", he wrote to a friend in 1968, "that I place it at the core of much of our domestic and international political, social, and economic difficulties."[19]

His opposition to Vietnam was intimately related to his long-standing apprehension over the acceleration of inflation. After the war ended, his concern deepened over the apparent incompatibility of high employment with price stability. He expressed his anxieties in letters in 1974 and 1975.

> I am not. . .sanguine about the present world malaise, the principal outward manifestation of which is worldwide inflation. In my more depressed moments I see the basic cause of persisting long-run inflation as being the infinite desires of human beings outrunning their finite willingness to defer present consumption for the sake of future benefits.[20]
>
> As a person who was influenced by Ortega y Gasset's *Revolt of the Masses* in his youth, I am beginning to have global forebodings. The essential principles of capitalism and of democracy are on a collision course, although the time of final impact approaches slowly.
>
> Or have I grown old and is my vision obscured? There hasn't been a president of the United States I could be enthusiastic about since I put on long pants, although I did like Kennedy as a person![21]

And, of course, he was indeed growing old, Marion as well. In the 1970s their health, which had not been robust, began to deteriorate further. Late in 1973 Marion entered the hospital for surgery; it was not successful, and she died on the operating table. They had been married almost fifty-three years.

Afterward, he continued to work, but without the same enthusiasm. He lunched often with Marriner Eccles, who by then made his home primarily in San Francisco. They had always gotten along well personally, despite frequent doctrinal disputes, and their mutual friendship became even

[19] Letter from Sproul to Robert V. Roosa, February 13, 1968.
[20] Letter from Sproul to Robert V. Roosa, June 25, 1974.
[21] Letter from Sproul to Robert V. Roosa, September 19, 1975.

warmer as they grew older. And he thought frequently of his years at the Federal Reserve Bank. "One of the things in my life which I cherish most", he wrote in a 1977 letter, "is that when I was at the Federal Reserve Bank of New York I earned the respect and became a friend of some younger men of superior ability who went on to great accomplishment."[22]

He gave his last scheduled talk to the Wells Fargo directors on February 21, 1978. Less than seven weeks later, on April 9, at the age of eighty-two years and one month, he died.

Following Marion's death, he had thought about ending his association with Wells Fargo because it was too demanding. However, he finally decided to continue because, as he wrote to a friend, "keeping in touch with current economic developments will help me in making the adjustments to life without Marion which I face. 'We have to struggle on, even if the idea of the ultimate pointlessness of everything hovers on the edge of our thoughts, even if we know that there will never be a final answer to man's questionings.'"[23]

[22] Letter from Sproul to Robert V. Roosa, March 16, 1977.
[23] Letter from Sproul to Robert V. Roosa, January 26, 1974.

Chapter 2

Monetary Policy and Inflation

Two principal themes were never far from the surface of Allan Sproul's thinking from early in his career until the very end. One was the need to exercise human judgment, with all its admitted imperfections, in the conduct of monetary policy. The other was the need to take meaningful action, monetary and otherwise, to prevent inflation.

This chapter contains six "papers" bearing on the subject of inflation, spanning almost a quarter century of his thinking (from 1951 to 1974). He was never insensitive to the attainment of other national economic objectives—such as high employment and balance-of-payments equilibrium—but in his view the goal of reasonable price stability was generally at least as important as any other objective and frequently more so. Indeed, he felt that, without price stability, the attainment of any other goals would be short-lived at best.

To that end, he on occasion advocated selective controls over consumer and mortgage credit (as during the Korean war) and flirted from time to time with various forms of Government intervention in the wage-bargaining and price-setting process. Monetary and fiscal policy, he felt, had to be aided and abetted by some form of "incomes policy"—not as a substitute for monetary and fiscal policy, but as a supplement—if there was to be any realistic hope of stopping the wage-price spiral. "So far as Government is concerned," he wrote to Secretary of the Treasury Henry Fowler in 1965 (in a letter reprinted below), "I have always argued that the stool we use to get the most milk from the economic cow should have three legs—fiscal policy, monetary policy, and wage-price policy."

When he came right down to the point, however, he could never really settle on a satisfactory form that such wage-price intervention should take. Although he advocated an incomes policy in principle, he could never find a version in practice that would be effective and at the same time be consistent with the preservation of the economic and political freedoms he so greatly cherished. Because of this conflict, he was forever on the horns of a dilemma with respect to approval or disapproval of Government involvement in private wage-price bargaining and decision making.

Of one thing, though, he was always certain: regardless of the stance of fiscal policy, or the presence or absence of an incomes policy, without courageous monetary policies there was no hope of stopping the momentum of inflation. Monetary policy, by itself, might not be sufficient to do the job, but it was definitely a necessary component of any genuine anti-inflationary policy. He could never take seriously anyone who urged an incomes policy as a *substitute* for a firm and vigorous monetary and fiscal policy.

As a general rule, the papers reprinted in each section of this book are presented in historical order. In this chapter, however, Sproul's 1968 talk on "Monetary Policy and Government Intervention" has been placed at the end of the chapter, since it gives his views in depth and serves as a capstone to the four relatively short letters and one brief talk which precede it. More effective anti-inflationary monetary and fiscal policies, he concluded, are not "the narrow concern of men who are more interested in financial sobriety than in social progress, more interested in the growth of our material resources than in the improvement of our environment, more interested in money than in people. These concerns are inextricably intertwined."

Letter to Winthrop W. Aldrich

November 7, 1951

Mr. Winthrop W. Aldrich, Chairman
The Chase Manhattan Bank
18 Pine Street
New York 15, N.Y.

Dear Winthrop:

I have been thinking about your talk on inflation at Austin, Texas, next week, and particularly about your statement that all that is needed is the courage to do the job. Perhaps I am a little sensitive on this point, having had some responsibility for monetary and credit policy in the anti-inflationary struggle. At any rate I thought I would jot down some notes for your consideration.

 1. Inflation can arise from a variety of causes even though the end result is too much money chasing too few goods.

 2. Inflation can arise from the push of increased costs as well as from the pull of increased demand.

 (a) It can hardly be avoided if wages often go up but never come down, and if all the fruits of increased productivity go to favorably situated workers and stockholders, none to consumers. Although our goal is a high level of employment, there must be the possibility of dismissal for the inefficient worker. Even full employment can't and shouldn't mean security for everyone in his present job, or preferred work in the place where the workers prefer to live.

 (b) Inflation will gain strength if we try to keep inefficient management afloat, and in destructive competition with efficient management, by the use of Government or Government-guaranteed credit. There must be the possibility of bankruptcy for the inefficient firm, large or small.

 3. Inflation can arise from a farm price policy which matches every rise in industrial wages and prices with increased support for farm prices. That is almost built-in inflation.

4. The principal elements of an anti-inflation program in a country such as the United States are not unknown. They embrace fiscal policy, debt management, credit policy and, in time of war or great defense programs, such direct controls as will channel essential and scarce materials into defense production, and prevent the development or continuance of a wage-price spiral.

All of these things must be working in the same direction and toward the same end if there is to be any chance of success in an economy in which the maintenance of a high level of production and employment is necessary to meet our domestic needs and our international responsibilities.

5. I am not trying to minimize the importance of credit policy nor the responsibilities of the monetary authorities. I believe that credit policy has a big role to play in combating inflation even though the doses of credit restraint must be homeopathic. And I believe that a central banking system, independent alike from narrow political control (or Treasury domination) and from private pressures, is essential. But if you are going to call for courage you must call on a lot of people—the executive branch of the Government from which leadership should come, the Congress which preaches economy and appropriates lavishly, the monetary authorities, the bankers and institutional investors, the labor unions, the businessmen who, for example, sponsor escalator clauses in labor contracts, the farmers who demand "parity" prices, and a lot of other people.

The problem is not merely a lack of courage on the part of Democrats, or of monetary authorities working alongside a Democratic administration, and I hope and expect that you won't present it as such. You probably had all this in mind but I thought it would do no harm to send you these notes.

Sincerely,

Allan Sproul

Letter to Alfred Hayes*

March 1, 1964

Dear Al:

Thank you for sending me so promptly the annual report of the Bank for 1963. It is a fine job; I thought the opening section "1963: Achievements and Unfinished Tasks" was particularly effective in its presentation of the economic position of the United States, nationally and internationally.

I have been glad to see, too, that it has not gone unnoticed, publicly, that the tenor of the report indicates that you are not a member of the chorus which has been singing "don't offset the tax cut by being stingy with credit". The underlying theme of the "sing along with Mitch" group seems to be that there is still slack in the economy and that, until the economy is operating at full capacity and some predetermined minimum rate of unemployment has been achieved, we must rely on "statesmanship on the part of business and labor" to protect us from inflationary pressures; that we have suffered enough from what is now becoming internationally labeled a "stop and go" monetary policy. This is a variation of the theme that we should not let our domestic economic aims be thwarted by unnecessary concern about the international balance of payments and the position of the dollar. It really suggests a flexible monetary policy which doesn't flex until the economy is about to burst or the dollar is about to bust, or both.

It was kind of dramatic and instructive that, on the day the annual report of the Bank was released, the Bank of England raised its discount rate. It would be stupid, of course, to restrict credit merely because there has been a relaxation of fiscal restraint on the economy, but surely the rationale of the use of fiscal policy as an economic stimulant must, in our present state, include permitting monetary policy greater leeway for dealing effectively with developments in our domestic affairs or our international position which threaten sustainable growth or currency collapse.

---

* President, Federal Reserve Bank of New York, 1956-75.

I think President Kennedy understood this. I am not at all sure that President Johnson understands it or that he is even really much interested in the rationale of fiscal and monetary policy. This may mean a troubled time for the System if inflationary pressures at home or another worsening of the balance of payments should call for monetary action. President Kennedy, partly because of the belief or suspicion among many businessmen that he was loose on Government spending and credit policy, was concerned to show that he was not an easy money crank, and his attitude toward the System reflected this concern. President Johnson, on the other hand, because he talks somewhat like a businessman and because of his recent budget performance (which contained at least the usual amount of budget legerdemain) has gained a lot of kudos in the banking and business community. It may be, therefore, that his political view of the role of monetary policy may be overlooked, in the months ahead, and a possible shield of the System may be lacking.

If the difficulty of such an attitude in high places is compounded by a mixed-up situation in the Board of Governors and in the Federal Open Market Committee (as Bill Martin has seemed to imply in recent conversations of which I have heard reports), there may be stirring times ahead. It is also true, I think, that the opinion that the System will not be willing or able to act, if and when action may be desirable, because of political pressures or internal differences, is already beginning to contribute to the view that an inflationary period lies ahead. If this view feeds on itself, it will help to bring about what it purports to fear. Your reminder that the System must be allowed to play its proper role in the changing mix of fiscal and monetary policy, therefore, is most constructive.

Sincerely,

Allan

Letter to Henry H. Fowler

December 1, 1965

The Honorable Henry H. Fowler
Secretary of the Treasury
Treasury Department
Washington, D.C.

Dear Mr. Secretary:

Please excuse the formality, but this is serious. When you kindly let me come in to see you two weeks ago, you gave me a copy of a talk you were going to make in Chicago and asked me to tell you what there was in it with which I might not agree.

I have read the talk and thought about it, and I have read the reports of talks which you have subsequently made, and it seems to me that we agree pretty completely on objectives but disagree on how best to attain these objectives under present circumstances. We both want a continuance of steady vigorous growth of the economy and a minimum of unemployment with generally stable prices. We both believe in a Government-business partnership working toward these objectives at all times and, especially, when our country is engaged in a war. I think we both agree that we can accommodate the demands of the war in Vietnam and that we have the capacity to meet its economic burdens without resort to measures which a global war might entail.

We disagree, in the circumstances of today, as to the means of assuring an effective partnership of Government, business, and labor in meeting our responsibilities. So far as Government is concerned, I have always argued that the stool we use to get the most milk from the economic cow should have three legs—fiscal policy, monetary policy, and wage-price policy. Our present position is one in which, as you say, most of the previous slack in the economy has been taken up and there are now upward pressures on wages and prices which should be restrained if we are to continue the healthy economic growth of the past five years. Recent budget estimates show that we are faced with increasing budget deficits, so that fiscal policy will be providing a stimulant rather than the restraint which is needed. Our wage-price policy is a jerry-built affair which will have increasing difficulty in meeting the requirements of such a policy in a situation of high employment and optimum use of productive capacity in many lines of business. But there is one power of Government, long established by the Congress with an effective Government agency charged with its execution, which I think is made to order for use in the present situation. That is general monetary policy.

Here a measure of restraint can be applied which will help to sift out marginal and speculative demands for credit, to relieve some of the upward pressures on wages and prices, and to offset some of the stimulant from the fiscal side which is not now appropriate. Yet, use of this power by the Federal Reserve System has been put under wraps by repeated public statements which are interpreted as a freeze on action with respect to the availability and cost of credit. Nor should the bearing of such action on our balance of payments be overlooked. It is neither necessary nor possible to try to bring into equilibrium interest rates in this country and in other money centers, in order to assert a favorable influence on—although certainly not to cure—the deficit in our balance of payments. The likelihood of a ratcheting upward of rates abroad has now decreased, some additional funds would stay home with higher rates here, and confidence here and abroad in our will to restrain inflationary pressures and to remain competitive in our own and foreign markets would be increased.

What all this adds up to is that I think the discount rate should be raised, the existing ceiling under Regulation Q should be raised, the availability of reserves should be reduced somewhat, and the prime rate of the commercial banks should be increased. You hold an opposite view. I think that, if there is ever going to be a time to use general monetary policy to restrain excesses in the economy and to contribute to sustained economic growth, this is it.

I am sorry that you have not been able to see it this way. But I am sure that you will not charge me with putting profits above patriotism in advocating it.

Yours sincerely,

Allan Sproul

Letter to Alfred Hayes

December 13, 1970

Dear Al:

Your statesmanlike talk to the Savings Bankers struck the right notes. I hope that your views will be influential in the formulation of the fiscal and monetary policies which will become clearer when the budget estimates and the economic reports to the Congress come along next month.

The President bothers me on a lot of counts. One count is his glibness on fiscal and monetary matters. His change from an initial position of balancing the unified federal budget to a position of balancing a full employment budget is too facile. The theoretical full employment budget has its place and attraction in the present state of the economy, but unless we have an expenditure ceiling which the Congress will accept and observe it also has its dangers. I am for it in theory, but I worry about it in practice.

The statement he made in New York recently about a commitment from Arthur Burns on monetary policy seemed to me to be disingenuous at best. I suspect that Burns may have said something to the effect that the Federal Reserve will continue to do its job, which is to meet the productive monetary needs of the economy at all times while trying to avoid adding to inflationary pressures. The President's statement, however, implied: (1) that monetary policy would become more aggressively easy, working along with a stimulative full employment budget policy to hasten economic recovery and a decline in unemployment without too many qualms about inflation, and (2) that Burns, personally, could deliver a binding commitment on future Federal Reserve action.

This sort of misunderstanding is one of the dangers of talking with presidents on such matters (shades of Truman).
They tend to hear what they want to hear, and they may
claim to have commitments from the Federal Reserve System
which have not been given, but which it is hard to deny
publicly without seeming to imply that the president is a liar
or an economic ignoramus. It is significant that Burns avoided this issue in his Los Angeles appearance, and concentrated on anti-inflation measures which might be taken, now
or soon, in support of fiscal and monetary policies.

A central banker's lot is not an easy one!

Sincerely,

Allan

Excerpts from the remarks of Allan Sproul at the Board of Directors Meeting, Wells Fargo Bank, San Francisco, California, April 16, 1974

In these remarks I do not want to quarrel with the overall forecast for economic activity during the rest of this year nor to enter into the debate on the particular means and methods of trying to make the forecast come true. The forecast is still the best we have at the moment, and it has achieved some momentum of its own through widespread acceptance. Differences in the prescriptions for helping to keep the economy on course are important but will not determine the outcome. No one of them is likely to be fully accepted and given political life, and they are all subject to modification in the light of future developments. Interest rates already have indulged in a temporary zig when they were supposed to be in a continuous zag.

The question which disturbs me is more fundamental. It is whether we are not being forced to grapple with a problem which is not only intractable but may be insoluble; whether within the limits of our political institutions and economic knowledge we can command a mixture of government intervention and market freedom which will provide an acceptable degree both of price stability and so-called full employment, especially if full employment always is the top priority. We have been trying to combine these two objectives, under the mandate of the Employment Act of 1946, for over a quarter of a century. And we have only come close when, in February 1966, our indexes showed a satisfactory rate of economic growth, with a 4 percent rate of unemployment and an inflation rate of 2 percent on an annual basis.

Ever since then we have been fighting a losing battle, with small victories on one front or the other but with major defeats overall. Prices and wages have risen in times of slackened demand as well as in times of active demand; in times of underutilization of our productive capacity as well as in times of overutilization. Unemployment has been above the level which had been given political blessing (commonly

4 percent of the civilian labor force) most of the time. And monetary and fiscal policies have been dragged in or moved in to validate the rising level of prices (and wages). An increasing public belief that our attempts to achieve an arbitrary unemployment goal (the meaning of our employment and unemployment statistics is still suspect in terms of the employment quality and availability of a substantial part of our population) has too often erred on the side of stimulating demand pressures, has widened public expectation of continuing inflation, and accentuated the bias toward inflation which already existed in our economy. It is easier to raise prices than to lower them; the average level of all prices seldom declines, and wage rates almost never go down.

More than anything else, it was this increasing expectation of continuing inflation, and the acceleration of inflation which such expectations fostered, which forced an administration which professed an abhorrence of wage-price controls, to resort to a wage-price freeze in August 1971. This action had a brief success as an emergency measure widely accepted on a temporary basis. Subsequent attempts to ease off into an institutionalized incomes policy failed, however, and are now headed toward emasculation if not abandonment.

If we have found out anything from this experience, it is that our economy under a system of government wage-price controls does not make the necessary adjustments in supply-demand relationships required by changing domestic and international conditions—changes in relative prices and relative wages, changes in technical progress, changes in the availability and use of natural resources, changes in public demands, and on and on.

Whatever acceptance the program had by business, which initially was surprisingly widespread, has evaporated. And it never had much acceptance by organized labor which is wedded to free collective bargaining, and the leverage which it provides to push up wages and benefits so long as government, in effect, is trying to guarantee "full employment", and management can expect to recoup increased costs by increasing prices.

And so we are pretty much back where we started, faced with an inflationary situation which we don't know how to check unless we are willing to run the risk of a further slowing down of economic growth and increased unemployment, which is a risk no one intrinsically desires and which the administration says it won't take.

My own view is that in a situation in which all choices are risky, priorities must be established to deal with the greater risk more firmly than with the lesser risk. And I believe that in our present situation curbing inflation should be our top priority. We have been in an upward surge of inflation without recent precedent except in time of war. Our fiscal and monetary policies should be directed toward checking that surge, not to provoke a recession but to prevent a continuing and possibly accelerating inflation which would lead to greater problems of reduced economic growth and increased unemployment than we now face. As Chairman Burns of the Board of Governors of the Federal Reserve System said recently, if rapid inflation continues this year, it could undermine confidence in the capacity of government to deal with the problem and seriously diminish our chances of regaining stable and broadly based prosperity.

There are those, however, who have become discouraged by recent failures in dealing with inflation and who have begun to seek radical solutions (on the Brazilian model). If you can't lick it, join it, they say. And then to protect as many as possible of those who may be hurt in the process, they suggest that escalator clauses be affixed to wages, pensions, long-term interest rates and contracts or wherever, which would compensate for increases in prices. This is another manifestation of the recurring search for some mechanical cure-all, or "cure-most", which would avoid the hazards of human fallibility in struggling to maintain the dynamic equilibrium of a complex society subject to the rational and irrational actions of millions of human beings. What price indexes might be chosen for the suggested compensatory adjustments to inflation in a democratic and complex economy such as the United States, what would be the fate of those parts of the economy which would not fit into the program, what would be the effect on our international relationships—the answers to these and other questions are not divulged.

We can leave such proposals to be threshed out in the academic groves. In the present state of our economic knowledge, and in our present circumstance, we must grapple with inflation with our existing monetary and fiscal powers. If this means temporary acceptance of a slower rate of economic growth than we desire, that is the price of previous excesses. We have enough built-in stabilizers in our economy to prevent a severe and prolonged recession—a depression. We have no built-in stabilizers to prevent inflation.

Talk before Business Economists Conference
Graduate School of Business Administration
University of Chicago, May 9, 1968

Monetary Policy and Government Intervention

The last time I addressed myself publicly and specifically to the subject of "Inflation: How Great An Issue?" was in an article which appeared in Fortune magazine in July 1959, when I still retained fresh memories of my experience as an official of the Federal Reserve System during the inflationary period following World War II. At that time I took a rather dim view of our ability to maintain the purchasing power of the dollar while hitching national politico-economic policy, by law, to the maintenance of maximum production, employment, and income, if we were not ready, willing, and able to curb the possible misuses and abuses of such a policy by government and by business, labor, agriculture, and a host of minor pressure groups. I ended my lament for the dollar by saying that, unless we committed ourselves to the hard things which would help eliminate upside rigidities and restore downside flexibility in costs and prices, the expectation and the actuality of rising costs and prices would persist, the one reinforcing the other. The only hedge I permitted myself was that deterioration of our international financial position might force or shock us into taking the necessary measures.

My gloomy assessment of the inflationary outlook was followed by a remarkable period of relative stability of prices accompanied by generally vigorous economic growth during the early sixties, precious little of which could be attributed to an adequate response to a deteriorating international position. In fact, we tended to comfort ourselves, as the deficit in the balance of payments persisted, with the thought that our international accounts eventually would be self-correcting if we continued to maintain a competitive international trading position in the private sector, notwithstanding the effects of heavy government spending abroad and the uncertainties of the ebb and flow of capital and credit. My confidence in my ability to discern the shape of things to come reached a new low.

If one lives long enough, however, and rides with a forecast which contemplates that human myopia, government shortcomings, and unforeseen events such as the Vietnam war are likely to thwart or deflect rational hopes and aspirations, you quite often turn out to be right eventually. Government intervention in economic affairs is accident prone—it seems to have an affinity to "Murphy's law—if it can fail, it will fail, and if it does fail, it will fail at the worst possible time and place".

Right now, at a time of national peril at home and abroad, our goal of maximum production and high employment, without inflation, has been placed beyond present reach. Inflationary pressures are in the ascendant. Our bright hopes of development of flexible fiscal policies to help counter economic fluctuations, which masqueraded for a time under the name of the "new economics", have been destroyed at least temporarily, and it has become questionable whether a government of divided powers such as ours can achieve this kind of fiscal flexibility. Monetary policy, deprived of the assistance of fiscal policy, perhaps assailed by inner doubts, and in the face of the frequent and large demands of deficit financing by the Federal Government, has lost much of its flexibility and has temporized with inflationary pressures while it has flirted with selective controls of credit and the international movement of funds. Attempts to devise and apply an incomes or wage-price policy through government guidelines have become a series of retreats, covered by ineffective government pleas for economic statesmanship on the part of organized labor and big business. Nor would a compulsory program promise better results, even if it were politically possible and privately tolerable. The problem of productivity which is the heart of the matter cannot be solved by wage-price controls; you cannot legislate labor-management cooperation for increased efficiency.

Whether we look at our domestic economy or our international financial relationships, then, there are ominous signs that the apparatus of government intervention in economic affairs is in disarray. We are being forced toward and into the use of selective and direct controls because we have allowed ourselves to be overtaken by events for which we have not prepared or have prepared inadequately.

Recent experience, if one deplores a proliferation of selective direct controls, is almost enough to throw one into the arms of Milton Friedman; to make one look for mechanical guides or free floating mechanisms to replace fallible human discretion in the guidance of economic intervention by government.

Let me give one or two examples which may serve to illustrate my thought. On the domestic side, we have seen how the administration of general monetary policy has been partially diverted from broad pervasive measures, which interfere as little as possible with the decisions of reasonably competitive markets, toward attempts to channel credit into the housing industry. By using the power to fix ceiling rates on the interest which banks can pay on savings and time deposits, and especially on large-denomination certificates of deposit, the authorities have sought to promote the competitive position of those nonbanking institutions which have been large investors in home mortgages. The government has a legitimate concern for the quality and cost of housing in the United States, but the source, availability, and cost of mortgage credit is only one aspect of the problem. Undue emphasis on this one aspect, particularly as it relates to general credit administration, serves to distract attention from a more deep-seated and persistent industrial sickness. Here is an industry of the greatest social and economic importance which suffers from fragmented operating units addicted to mediocrity or worse in subdivision development, guild-like practices of the building trades unions relating to the use of equipment and materials and the training of apprentices, municipal building codes which are often obsolete in terms of today's technology and which vary widely from place to place, and mortgage instruments which seem to be less than perfect for purposes of long-term lending of potentially short-term money. As a social priority, government intervention in and subvention of the housing industry should be more direct, and should take account of the whole state of the industry. It should not rely so heavily on the evasive method of selective credit control which may pervert general monetary policy, while it largely ignores basic defects in the industry itself.

On the international side, we have had the actions which government has taken to control the outflow of private capital and credit from the United States, in its attempts to right the international balance of payments without paying adequate attention to government outflows and to the use of general fiscal and monetary policies to help achieve the objective. The interest equalization tax on purchases of certain foreign securities was proposed as a temporary measure in 1963, enacted in 1964, and is still with us five years later in expanded form. We are now in the fourth year of voluntary and mandatory regulation of bank lending and direct investment abroad, there has been a suggestion that such controls be made permanent and more detailed, and the executive branch of the government recently burned its fingers trying to get the Congress to clamp down on tourist travel to certain foreign countries. Each one of these selective direct controls has been precipitated by a crisis situation, and has served as cover for the fact that, at the core of the problem of the balance of payments, have been our increasing military expenditures abroad and our lax fiscal-monetary policies at home, which have finally eroded our competitive trading position and which have progressively weakened confidence in the dollar and in the whole international system of fixed parity convertible currencies.

I deplore most selective, direct controls of the economy by government because they smack of totalitarian methods, and because I do not think they ever have or possibly can equal the performance of private markets, imperfect though such markets may be, in organizing and operating an advanced, complex economy. I deplore them because of their tendency to proliferate and to live beyond the crisis which brings them into being, until they have invaded and destroyed healthy organisms in the private market. I deplore them because of their insidious effect on those who try to operate the levers of control and are seduced into seeking greater and greater power because of the imperfect performance of the powers they already have. Finally, I deplore them because so often they represent an attempt to paper over cracks in the economic structure and defects in general economic policies, which we haven't had the wit or the will to attack directly. I am reminded of a World War II regulation which said that "the Department of Agriculture and the War Production Board have issued an order cutting 75 percent of the jelly bean production to preserve sugar. The War Production Board previously stopped the manufacture of chocolate Easter eggs and chocolate rabbits." This resounding order caused Margaret Fishback, a mistress of light verse, to write:

Farewell to chocolate Easter rabbits
And other pleasant peacetime habits.
Egg rolling on the White House lawn
That springtime revel too is gone.
And although jelly beans remain
They're definitely on the wane.
While those who color eggs for baby
Will eat them, and I don't mean maybe.

At the other end of the spectrum of opinions on government intervention in economic affairs, and more specifically such intervention by way of fiscal-monetary policy, I cannot accept the view of those who want to eliminate or drastically reduce the element of flexibility and discretion in these matters by prescribing some norm for intervention, to be followed without deviation through time and circumstance. Getting a little closer to my assigned subject, "Monetary Policy and Government Intervention", I dislike this prescription, particularly, because it tends to deny the direct importance of fiscal policy and to exalt the importance of monetary policy in smoothing cyclical fluctuations of the economy. Massive statistical compilations have been assembled— Friedman and Schwartz, *Monetary History of the United States, 1867-1960,* has 700 pages plus appendixes—in an attempt to show that the rate of change of the money supply is the overriding determinant of fluctuations in business and in national income and prices; that to the extent that the central bank can control the money supply it can control the business cycle with minimal deviations in the time lag between cause and effect; and that the best policy for the central bank is to maintain a steady rate of growth of the money supply at a rate which corresponds roughly to the growth of the economy's productive capacity. In their use of discretion, proponents of this view suggest, the monetary authorities of the United States have most often been wrong in the direction or timing of their actions, and when they seemed to be right it was usually by mistake.

I used to rely on a quotation from Paul Samuelson to express my view of this position. He once wrote concerning it that "a definitive mechanism which is to run forever after, by itself, involves a single act of discretion which transcends, in both its arrogance and its capacity for potential harm, any repeated acts of foolish discretion that can be imagined". More specific refutation of the money supply thesis, insofar as the asserted prevailing relationships between monetary cycles and cycles of general business are concerned, is not lacking, however. Just recently an article appeared in the *Monthly Review* of the Federal Reserve Bank of New York, written by Richard Davis of the Bank's economic research department, which examined the relevant statistics and concluded that the relationship between the two kinds of cycles has certain attributes of a chicken and egg relationship, but does not provide real support for the view that the behavior of money is the predominant determinant of fluctuations in business activity. At the same time, the study finds that the historical relationships between cycles in money and in business cannot be used, accurately, to demonstrate that discretionary monetary policy is, in its effects, so long delayed and so uncertain in its timing as to be an unsatisfactory countercyclical weapon. The coincidence of the results of this careful piece of research with my own pragmatic views makes it easy for me to accept Mr. Davis's findings.

I do not want to seem cavalier in dismissing the idea of automatic guides or formulae for government intervention in economic affairs. I believe, however, that, except for the intellectual enjoyment of debating the issue, the idea is sterile in the present state of our economic knowledge of where we are, how we got here, and where we are going. The live issue today is whether we are going to continue to strive for better performance in the use of general and pervasive discretionary powers of government intervention to deal with a variety of complex economic situations, or whether we are going to become enmeshed in a thicket of selective controls. I suggest that we can preserve more of the advantages of decision by the private market if we follow the former course.

Where does all this leave me? I have said that discretionary government intervention in our economic affairs by generally pervasive fiscal-monetary action has failed us rather badly during the past three years, the period of our increasing military involvement in Southeast Asia. At the same time, I have rejected the idea of more specific and selective government intervention in our economic system, and I have rejected the idea of automatic guides or controls of such government action. Well, it leaves me where anyone is likely to be left in dealing with human affairs through government agencies—considerably short of perfection but not without hope for a better future. I still think that the government's role as intervenor in our economic life should be by way of flexible, discretionary, contracyclical fiscal and monetary policies with, perhaps, an assist from a continuing educational program with respect to the relationship between national and individual productivity and real income, hoping that at some future time we might be able to establish conditions which will be favorable to a general and viable incomes or wage-price policy which will work in periods of high employment and strong consumer demand. I do not think that we can do better than this, at least until economists know more than they now know about future economic developments, and until government and community acceptance of what they know is greater than it now is.

To fortify our hopes for a better future, however, we must be critical of our past failures. We must refute the dictum of an old colleague of mine that what separates man from the animals is that the animals learn by experience. We have to admit that our performance since mid-1965, when we began the tragic escalation of our military involvement in Vietnam, has not been good at home and that internationally it has brought us close to disaster. At the core of our failure has been our approach to the economic demands of the war. We bemused ourselves with aggregates, that the war and its related costs would only demand a small percentage of the gross national product, and that we could massively enlarge our output of goods and services without strain, even though the new demands were being injected into an economy already operating in the upper range of its rated capacity. We slipped and slithered into a larger and more costly war than we had anticipated, while we refused to admit that because of the war we might have to slight serious domestic needs and problems, that we might have to demand sacrifices of more than chewing gum by the civilian population, and that we might have to cut back some of our other government commitments abroad to avoid continued weakening of our international financial position.

It was a time of testing of the so-called "new economics". It was a time of testing whether we could not only speed up the economy with tax cuts, increased government spending, and easy money, but also whether we could slow it down with tax increases, reduced government spending, and credit restraint. A coordinated, two-way fiscal-monetary policy was needed, and it failed to come through the barbed wire entanglements of our governmental procedures. The executive branch of the government made some of the right motions with respect to fiscal policy in fiscal 1965-66, but never with enough vigor and follow-through to impress the Congress or the public. At the same time the executives used influence and the pressures of high office to deter the monetary authorities from reducing the availability and increasing the cost of credit, so as to keep demand from pressing too heavily against the upper limits of supply. When the monetary authorities finally applied the brakes without the assistance of adequate fiscal action, a banking crisis threatened—the "crunch" of the fall of 1966—and signs of a possible business decline appeared. This provided a more congenial occasion for government intervention and a coordinated fiscal-monetary policy. Tax incentives for investment, which had been removed, were quickly restored, government spending was speeded up, and easy money again became the order of the day. On the whole, the response of the economy was enlivening, and it resumed its upward course but, unfortunately, unit costs were now beginning to rise more widely, prices were rising more rapidly, the deficit in the federal budget was seen to be getting badly out of control, and the international monetary system which leans so heavily on the dollar was being seriously frayed by the continued substantial deficit in our balance of payments and the methods we were using to try to correct it.

Again the need was for a coordinated policy of fiscal and monetary restraint which, while it could not erase the inflationary pressures already in being, and in prospect as demands for large wage increases multiplied, could help restrain the further excesses which might otherwise develop. Again the executive was moving toward fiscal action in the tax side, having proposed a surtax increase of 6 percent and then having raised the ante to 10 percent, a display of fiscal resolve which was weakened by accompanying increases in proposed federal expenditures. Again the monetary authorities watched and waited to see how the fiscal cat would jump while the cat drowsed on the Congressional hearth. There was the distressing debate over whether the Executive or the Congress should appear to be responsible for an increase in taxes and a reduction of expenditures in an election year. There was the resort to statistical aggregates to support the view that the nation's productive plant and labor resources were not overextended, even though increased prices were adulterating the apparent rate of economic growth. There was the specious claim that these increases in prices were of the cost-push variety and therefore not amenable to fiscal-monetary action, although cost-push soon depends on demand-pull for continued life.

The result was no significant fiscal action, a worsening budgetary situation, and a monetary policy which remained unduly expansive, even though interest rates rose to historically high levels, until a near breakdown of confidence in the dollar and in the international monetary system precipitated the beginnings of a less extravagant program. In brief, fiscal-monetary policy was found lacking, and again we approached the boundaries of unsustainable, unbalanced economic growth, accompanied by increased unit costs and increased prices, again we dissipated opportunities to improve our balance-of-payments position and to protect the international value of the dollar by preserving our competitive stance, and again we teetered in the direction of a widening circle of direct, selective controls.

If one cause of this current failure, in the important matter of government intervention in economic affairs, is to be elevated above all others, I would say that, aside from a general failure in determining national priorities, it has been the failure of coordination between the executive and the legislative branches of government in matters of fiscal-monetary policy. Walter Heller has said that what is new in the "new economics" is that for the first time two presidents—President Kennedy achieving the breakthrough and President Johnson consolidating our position—have pressed the lessons and tools of modern economics into full-time use in national policy. Unfortunately, the executive pressure faltered when restraint was desirable, and the Congress hadn't mastered the lesson or hadn't been given the tools, and Wilbur Mills wasn't consulted or convinced.

I have no starry-eyed plans for reforming the organization of the Congress, nor for changing the committee and sub-committee arrangements and the ordinary procedures of the Appropriations Committee and the Ways and Means Committee of the House of Representatives, and I recognize that the role of the Executive in the area of fiscal policy involves Constitutional questions of political power. If, however, we are eventually to achieve success in using a small part of the government's spending and taxing powers alongside monetary policy, as a constructive and moderating influence on the short-run fluctuations of business, the Congress and the Executive will have to devise a better method than now exists for mutual appraisal of the strategy and tactics of flexible contracyclical fiscal action, and a better means than now exists of reaching timely decisions in accord with national and international economic needs. If we really want to use a mixture of flexible fiscal and monetary policies in promoting sustainable economic growth, maximum employment, price stability, and international balance, it should not take years from the time the executive proposes a temporary increase (or a decrease) in taxes to reach a legislative decision on the proposal. That is a contribution to confusion and disorder in our economic affairs which we cannot afford at this critical stage of our national life.

Let there be no mistake. Emphasis on improved fiscal-monetary performance by government is not the narrow concern of men who are more interested in financial sobriety than in social progress, more interested in the growth of our material resources than in the improvement of our environment, more interested in money than in people. These concerns are inextricably intertwined. Right now, in a significant sense, achievement of our social and environmental goals, as well as our national and international economic well-being, have become fiscal and financial hostages of the race between de-escalation of the war in Vietnam and escalation of the domestic war against urban blight, poverty, and racial discrimination. If we do not regain control of the federal budget, and if we are not able to devise some means of coordinating flexible fiscal-monetary policies, we shall be risking all our long-term economic and social objectives, and weakening the defenses of our national security.

Chapter 3

Postwar Treasury-Federal Reserve Conflict and the Accord

The postwar dispute between the Treasury and the Federal Reserve, culminating in their famous 1951 "Accord", was discussed at some length in the introductory chapter of this book. The first of Allan Sproul's papers reproduced in the present chapter is the only full-length treatment of that episode he ever committed to print. He wrote it in 1964, and even then he probably would not have done so except for the urging of Alfred Hayes, his successor as president of the New York Reserve Bank, who asked that he write it for a special issue of the Bank's *Monthly Review* commemorating the fiftieth anniversary of the Federal Reserve System.

That article is followed by six letters, four written in the months or days prior to the Accord and two written more than ten years later. The four letters written shortly before the Accord recapture the sense of immediacy and urgency that was in the air at the time. They are to Robert T. Stevens, Chairman of the Board of Directors of the Federal Reserve Bank of New York; C.F. Cobbold, Governor of the Bank of England; Thomas B. McCabe, Chairman of the Board of Governors of the Federal Reserve System; and James E. Shelton, President of the American Bankers Association. However, there is some question whether the letter to Shelton was ever mailed; there is a notation "Not Sent" on the carbon copy in the Bank's files. In any case, it is a mystery how he ever found time to write such lengthy letters in late February 1951, when negotiations with the Treasury were at their peak.

The two letters written many years later, to Murray J. Rossant, then of the *New York Times,* are typical Allan Sproul post-1956 letters: lively, informative, and composed with a flair few could equal.

The chapter's introductory article on the Accord, written for the Bank's *Monthly Review*, illustrates Sproul's typical thoroughness. He begins the story that ends with the 1951 Accord not in 1941 or 1942, as most would, but rather in 1917 and 1918. And, just as typically, he does not stop with the Accord itself but goes on to draw from the experience the many lessons he sees it as providing for the future.

One of these lessons is that the Congress should "include a reference to price stability among the general guides to economic well-being in the preamble of the Employment Act, and to add a general directive with respect to price stability and the international position of the dollar to the Federal Reserve Act". Time has validated the wisdom of these recommendations.

But in no sense did he view the Accord as a "victory" for the Federal Reserve over the United States Government. "The Federal Reserve challenge to the Treasury's assertion of dominance in the area of their overlapping responsibilities", he concluded, "had its ultimate justification in the achievement of coequal status in these matters, and not as an assertion of a false independence. The Federal Reserve does not have, never has had, and never has claimed to have an independence in monetary affairs which divorces it from the general economic policies of the Government."

From *Monthly Review* of the Federal Reserve
Bank of New York, November 1964

The "Accord"—A Landmark in the First Fifty Years of the Federal Reserve System

Personal recollections of the history of institutions may range widely, following the broad avenue of the development of the institution itself, or the high road of the careers of individuals who served it, or they may focus on episodes which stand out in historical perspective as having a special significance. Such an episode in the history of the first fifty years of the Federal Reserve System is the web of events which found its denouement in the "Accord" of the Treasury and the Federal Reserve System in March 1951.

Having chosen to write about this controversial episode, because of special familiarity with it, I faced certain hazards which I have tried to avoid. One such hazard is that episodes of historical significance do not spring into being without a past and, inevitably, they have a future. So it is with the "Accord"; its roots go deep into the past of the Federal Reserve System and its influence is still being felt and its results are still being challenged. Yet, in an article such as this, if one is to avoid the trap of trying to write a history of the Federal Reserve System in a few thousand words, it is possible only to brush over the past of the "Accord" and touch only lightly on its future. A second hazard is that, in treating an episode in which one has participated, there is a tendency to embrace the benefits of hindsight. Recourse to records written at the time, and not since "improved", has helped me to avoid this hazard, I hope. But even if the advantages of hindsight are eliminated in this way, there remains the fact that most of the contemporary records I have consulted are the records of individuals or groups who were in the contending forces and only on one side—my side. I have had to try to avoid the hazard that my recollections, refreshed by a reading of written records, are subject to institutional and personal bias.

A fundamental cause of the controversy which led to the "Accord" was the growth in the importance of the overlapping responsibilities of the Treasury and the Federal Reserve during the years 1914-51. On the one side, the deficit financing of two world wars had made the management and cost of the Federal debt a matter of major economic and administrative concern, and the proliferation of Government securities of various maturities brought the Treasury to the market, for financing and refinancing, with increasing frequency. On the other side, the development of credit policy as one of the primary means of Government influence on the total economy, and the open market techniques which the monetary authorities evolved to discharge their responsibilities under law, meant that an overlapping area was created in which understanding and accommodation took the place of rigid legislative directives.

The first sprouting of the conflict inherent in such a situation appeared when the young Federal Reserve System was plunged into the problem of financing the participation of the United States in World War I. The then Secretary of the Treasury notified the Federal Reserve, early in 1917, of his desire to float an issue of certificates of indebtedness at a rate well below the market, which meant that the issue would have to be bought by the Federal Reserve Banks. Subsequently, the Secretary "undertook not to unload anything further on the Federal Reserve Banks, certainly not without notice, and in consideration of his attitude in the matter it was agreed that every effort should be made to bring about a satisfactory organization for shifting Treasury requirements to member banks and, through them, to the public".[1] A working entente was arranged by the System and the Treasury and, eventually, preferential discounting arrangements and preferential discount rates were established to facilitate Treasury financing through the banks of the country. These arrangements—the "bank-borrow-and-buy policy"—persisted for a year after the armistice in November 1918, at the insistence of the Treasury, and were an increasing source of friction between the Treasury and the System as inflationary pressures built up in the postwar economy. The

---

[1] *The Federal Reserve System* by H. Parker Willis (New York, 1923), pp. 1117-18.

System, in the euphemistic words of the *Annual Report of the Federal Reserve Board for 1920,* was prepared during 1919 to "resort to the well-known method of advancing the rate of discount, as soon as Treasury exigencies permitted".

Perhaps the Federal Reserve System further mingled the areas of responsibility in 1937-38, when the fledgling Federal Open Market Committee, created by the Banking Act of 1935, announced in April 1937 that "with a view to exerting its influence toward orderly conditions in the money market. . . it was prepared to make open market purchases of United States Government securities, for the account of the Federal Reserve Banks, in such amounts and at such times as may be desirable". Since Treasury bills and other short-term Treasury paper had already become bellwethers of the money market, this was an acceptance of responsibility for orderly conditions in the Government securities market. In fact, the *Annual Report of the Federal Reserve Bank of New York for the Year 1938* stated that "the open market operations in which this bank participated during the past year were not undertaken primarily with a view to affecting the reserve position of member banks, but rather with a view of exercising an influence toward the maintenance of orderly conditions in the market for Government securities".

This assumption by the credit authorities of a measure of responsibility for maintaining orderly conditions in the Government securities market hardened into a compact with the Treasury for the maintenance of a "pattern of rates" in that market to facilitate the financing of the United States participation in World War II. It was recognized by the parties to the compact that, insofar as it was politically and economically possible, the war should be financed out of taxes and that, for the rest, borrowing from nonbank investors (borrowing of savings) would be preferable to borrowing from the commercial banks. It was also recognized, however, that a substantial residue of borrowing would have to be done through the banks, and that this would involve an increase in the money supply (and in the liquidity of the economy) which would not be matched by an increase in goods and services available for civilian use. There was an inevitable inflationary factor in war financing, which was held in check but not removed by direct controls, such as materials priorities and price ceilings. At the time that this general approach to the problems of financing the war was adopted, it was also agreed that, to the extent the Treasury had to borrow from the banks, it should borrow at stable, not rising, rates of interest such as the financing methods of World War I had produced. This led to the establishment of a fixed "pattern of rates" which ranged from $\frac{3}{8}$ percent on ninety-day Treasury bills to 2½ percent for 20- to 25-year Government bonds (excluding Savings Bonds). As a by-product of this pegging of prices of Government securities, the initiative with respect to the creation of reserve credit was shifted from the Federal Reserve to the member banks.

In the reconversion period, at the end of the war in 1945, the problem facing the Federal Reserve System was how to proceed, and at what speed, to recapture from the banks of the country this initiative, and to restore the ability of the Federal Reserve Banks to place a price upon reserve credit and a check on its availability which could be varied to meet changes in economic circumstances. The Treasury, which had a proper concern for the functioning of the Government securities market, which had become habituated to the convenience of the method used to finance the war, which still had the problems of rolling over the war-swollen debt, and which was dubious of the scope left for a flexible monetary policy in the existing circumstances, was reluctant to abandon support prices and a "pattern of rates" for Government securities. In a situation of overlapping responsibilities and on the basis of seniority in the Washington hierarchy, the Treasury assumed the role of final decision. The System wished to discontinue before the end of 1945 its preferential discount rate on Government securities maturing within one year. Treasury acquiescence was not forthcoming until April 1946. From the closing months of 1945, all through 1946, the System was pressing for an end of its artificially low buying rate—$\frac{3}{8}$ percent— on ninety-day Treasury bills, but the Treasury would not agree until July 1947.

These small changes, important in themselves in terms of improving the structure of interest rates, were even more important as an indication of the intention of the Federal Reserve System gradually to restore its control over bank reserves and their availability. It was deemed to be an inevitable consequence of the great wartime increase in the money supply and in the total liquidity of the economy (of business, of consumers, and of the banking system) that inflationary pressures would assert themselves in time, and from time to time, as direct economic controls were removed. An appropriate credit policy would require restraint in the creation of additional bank reserves and would result in increases in short-term interest rates, including rates on short- and intermediate-term Government securities.

The hesitations and refusals of the Treasury meant that the defrosting of the wartime "pattern of rates" took place distressingly slowly, and then only in steps to a higher fixed rate curve ending with the 2½ percent long-term Government bonds. The supported rate of ⅞ percent on one year Treasury obligations was not raised to 1 percent until August 1947, to 1⅛ percent in November 1947, and to 1¼ percent in October 1948. The discount rates of the Federal Reserve Banks had to be kept in line with these rates, and were raised equally slowly from 1 percent to 1¼ percent in January 1948 and to 1½ percent in August 1948.

A slight business recession beginning in the fall-winter of 1948-49 provided an opportunity to emphasize the change which was gradually taking place in credit policy and, it was thought, in debt management. An official statement was published, couched in terms of the credit relaxation appropriate to a business downturn, that the "pattern of rates" had finally been abandoned. This was the statement issued on June 28, 1949:

> *The Federal Open Market Committee, after consultation with the Treasury, announced today that, with a view to increasing the supply of funds available in the market to meet the needs of commerce, business*

and agriculture, it will be the policy of the Committee to direct purchases, sales and exchanges of Government securities by the Federal Reserve Banks with primary regard to the general business and credit situation. The policy of maintaining orderly conditions in the Government security market, and the confidence of investors in Government bonds will be continued. Under present conditions the maintenance of a relatively fixed pattern of rates has the undesirable effect of absorbing reserves from the market at a time when the availability of credit should be increased.

Unfortunately, the acquiescence of the Treasury in the making of this statement by the Federal Open Market Committee was not meant to embrace a policy of flexibility in credit availability and interest rates, except when the flexibility was on the downside. As the economic climate changed and business moved up from the trough of recession, the System-Treasury debate over the coordination of debt management and credit policy resumed.

The persisting differences between the two agencies, of course, had not gone unnoticed in the Congress and in the public press. A subcommittee on Monetary Credit and Fiscal Policies (Chairman, Senator Douglas of Illinois), of the Joint Committee on the Economic Report, held hearings during the latter part of 1949 and, subsequently, made a report to its parent committee which discussed monetary and debt management policies and took special cognizance of the dispute between the Treasury and the Federal Reserve System. Among other things, it recommended ''that an appropriate, flexible and vigorous monetary policy, employed in coordination with fiscal and other policies, should be one of the principal methods used to achieve the purposes of the Employment Act [of 1946]''. And it went on to recommend, as a means of promoting monetary and debt management policies that would contribute most to the purposes of the Employment Act ''. . .that Congress by joint resolution issue general instructions to the Federal Reserve and Treasury regarding the objectives of monetary and debt management policies and the division of authority over those policies. These instructions need not, and in our opinion should not, be detailed: they should accomplish their purpose if they provide, in effect that, (1) in determining and administering policies relative to money, credit and management of the Federal debt, the Treasury and the Federal Reserve shall be guided primarily by considerations relating to the effects on employment, production, purchasing power and price levels, and such policies shall be consistent with and shall promote the purpose of the Employment Act of 1946; and (2) it is the will of Congress that the primary power and responsibility for regulating the supply, availability and cost of credit in general shall be vested in the duly constituted authorities of the Federal Reserve System, and that Treasury actions relative to money, credit and transactions in the Federal debt shall be made consistent with the policies of the Federal Reserve."[2] The press, on the whole, also was favorable to the position of the Federal Reserve. Bankers, insofar as they expressed themselves, were reluctant to take sides.

The unfortunate failure of the Treasury and the Federal Reserve to find common ground for meeting the responsibilities delegated to them by the Congress, where their fields of responsibility overlapped, was now approaching a climax. The economy was rapidly recovering from the slight downturn of 1949, when the outbreak of hostilities in Korea, in June 1950, "transformed the tone and the tempo of American economic life".[3] An already buoyant economy became surcharged with inflationary pressures; anticipatory spending by consumers and business reflected expectations of increased Government spending and Government demand

[2] It should be noted that one member of the subcommittee, Congressman Patman, stated that these proposals did not make the Federal Reserve sufficiently responsible to the Executive Department of the Federal Government and that the Joint Committee in its reference to these recommendations of the subcommittee recommended "further careful study".

[3] Federal Reserve Bank of New York, *Thirty-sixth Annual Report for the Year Ended December 31, 1950*, p. 5

for materials for military purposes; commodity prices were advancing rapidly; bank loans were rising, including business loans, as well as consumer loans and mortgage loans. Confronting this situation, President Truman, in a message to the Congress on July 19, 1950 concerning the Korean crisis and the defense program, called for primary reliance upon strong fiscal and credit measures to reduce the volume of private purchasing power competing with the Government for available goods and services. And, in his midyear Economic Report (July 26, 1950) there was this statement: "First of all for the immediate situation, we should rely in major degree upon fiscal and credit measures. . .the more prompt we are with these general measures the less need there will be for direct controls. . . ."

So far as the Federal Reserve was concerned, these statements of overall national policy confirmed its view of what it should be doing to help counteract the forces of inflation, not only by way of selective controls of consumers and mortgage credit but, more important, by general credit measures without which selective controls would not be effective. The Federal Reserve view, reaffirmed and reinforced in the light of the Korean crisis, had been given to the Secretary of the Treasury earlier in July, when it was stated that the System could not maintain the existing rate structure in the Government securities market while going forward with the general policy of regaining control of the initiative with respect to bank reserves which it deemed essential; either short-term rates would have to rise or the long-term rate would have to come down, and both from the standpoint of countering inflationary pressures and correcting an artificial interest rate structure, it preferred the first alternative. The Treasury reply counseled delay until the situation became clearer, and emphasized that the nation was waiting to learn what domestic programs might be needed in order to utilize the full strength of the country in national defense. The Federal Reserve System believed that the messages of the President had now answered the question.

The action question, which remained on the agenda of the Federal Open Market Committee, was what contribution it would make to the general program in its sphere of primary responsibility; what it would do about making further reserve funds available to the banking system in an inflationary situation which could quickly become critical and in which the effectiveness of moderate general credit measures of restraint would depend upon the promptness of their use. The Federal Reserve felt that it was under the compulsions of statutory responsibility to meet a present danger, and that it had exhausted the possibilities of devising a mutually agreeable program with the Treasury which would have permitted credit policy and debt management to go forward in tandem.

So it was, on August 18, 1950, the Board of Governors of the Federal Reserve System approved an increase in the discount rate of the Federal Reserve Bank of New York from 1½ percent to 1¾ percent (effective August 21), which had been held in abeyance for about a month, and the Federal Open Market Committee adopted a general policy of making reserves less readily available to the banks of the country, and then informed the Treasury of what it was doing. Up to this point, the Federal Reserve had presented its views concerning an appropriate combination of credit policy and debt management to the Treasury; the Treasury had decided what it was going to do and had then informed the Federal Reserve; and the Federal Reserve had followed along, attempting to adjust its open market operations, as best it could, to the debt management decisions of the Treasury. The August 1950 decision reflected the Federal Reserve's belief that the facts of the economic situation and the general economic program of the Government demanded that it break out of that pattern.

Advice of the actions taken was immediately given, orally, to the Secretary of the Treasury by the Chairman and Vice Chairman of the Federal Open Market Committee (afternoon of August 18, 1950). A delayed response without further conference came within the hour. The Treasury had decided to announce its September-October refunding— a $13.5 billion operation— at once, maintaining the existing rate of 1¼ percent for one-year obligations. (The actual offering was a thirteen-month note.) The result was an issue which was a market failure—the Federal Reserve had to purchase the larger part, upward of 80 percent—of the maturing securities in order to make sure that the Treasury would not have an embarrassing cash redemption. At the same time, as an offset to the effect of these purchases on bank reserves, the Federal Reserve sold other securities from its portfolio at prices and yields in line with its actions on discount rates and open market policy.

There followed a period of confused and confusing attempts to reestablish a working formula for coordinating debt management and credit policy. The President of the United States was early brought into the embarrassing dispute by the Treasury. A temporary truce was evolved which permitted time to observe the results of the actions taken by the Federal Reserve and, in November 1950, there was a fairly amicable agreement embracing credit policy and the Treasury refunding of its December and January maturities with a 1¾ percent five-year note. As it turned out, the new note did not fare well and, in terms of the amount of the maturing issues which the Federal Reserve had to buy and the amount which the market redeemed for cash, the financing was not a success.

The Treasury evidently felt that it had been let down, and that some public statement had to be made to restore confidence in the Government securities market. In a speech at New York, on January 18, 1951, the Secretary of the Treasury declared that "the delusion that fractional changes in interest rates can be effective in fighting inflation must be dispelled from our minds"; that "any increase in the 2½ percent rate for long-term Government securities would seriously upset existing securities markets"; and that "the Treasury Department had concluded, after a joint conference with President Truman and Chairman McCabe of the Federal Reserve Board, that refunding and new money issues of the Treasury will be financed within the pattern of that rate". This attempted reestablishment of a "pattern of rates" in Government financing, and the implication of a commitment by the Federal Reserve to support the 2½ percent long-term rate on new as well as outstanding issues of Treasury securities, was immediately challenged, most notably by Marriner Eccles, a member and former Chairman of the Board of

Governors, in testimony at a hearing of the Joint Committee on the Economic Report which was then in session.

Amid a rising volume of public comment on, and Government concern over, the differences between the Treasury and the Federal Reserve System, it was announced on January 31, 1951, that President Truman had asked members of the Federal Open Market Committee to come to the White House that afternoon. There followed a bizarre exchange of contradictory reports on what had taken place at the meeting. A White House press secretary said that the Federal Reserve had pledged its support to President Truman in maintaining the stability of Government securities as long as the emergency lasted. A Treasury spokesman said that the White House statement meant that the market for Government securities would be stabilized at their present levels and that these levels would be maintained during the emergency. These press reports, which left a cloud of doubt as to what had happened at the White House meeting, were given official sanction in a letter from the President to Chairman McCabe which was released to the press on February 1, 1951. In it the President wrote, "your assurance that you would fully support the Treasury defense financing program, both as to its refunding and new issues, is of vital importance to me. As I understand it, I have your assurance that the market on Government securities will be stabilized and maintained at present levels in order to assure the successful financing requirements and to establish in the minds of the people confidence concerning Government credit."

This was at variance with what the Federal Open Market Committee believed had been said and done at the White House meeting. In a memorandum prepared immediately after the meeting, the Federal Reserve recorded that there had been no references to recent disputes with the Treasury; and that at no time had the President indicated that he had in mind support, or a pledge of support, of the financing program recently outlined by the Secretary of the Treasury (January 18, 1951 at New York). Shocked by the public letter of the President to Chairman McCabe, Governor Eccles released the Federal Reserve record to the press on his personal responsibility, on February 3, 1951.

An intolerable situation had been created in which, as the Federal Open Market Committee said in a letter to the President on February 7, 1951, "You as President of the United States and we as members of the Federal Open Market Committee have unintentionally been drawn into a false position before the American public—you as if you were committing us to a policy which we believe to be contrary to what we all truly desire, and we as if we were questioning you and defying your wishes as the chief executive of the country in this critical period". The letter went on to say that "in accordance with our assurance to you, we shall seek to work out with the Secretary of the Treasury as promptly as possible a program which is practical, feasible and adequate in the light of the defense emergency, which will safeguard and maintain public confidence in the values of outstanding Government bonds and which, at the same time, will protect the purchasing power of the dollar".

Concurrently with the sending of this letter to the President, a meeting of the Chairman and Vice Chairman of the Federal Open Market Committee was held with Senate leaders of the Banking and Currency Committee, a subcommittee of which had been named to inquire into the Treasury-Federal Reserve controversy. The general tenor of the senatorial advice was that it was no time for feuding and no time for a Congressional hearing, but a time for the Treasury and the Federal Reserve to try again to compose their differences. The same advice was given by the Senator Chairman of the Committee on the Joint Economic Report, the following day.

This counsel from members of the Congress, from which the Federal Reserve System derives its authority and powers, coincided with the wishes of the Federal Open Market Committee, which on the same day (February 7, 1951) that it had written to the President drafted a letter to the Secretary of the Treasury expressing a desire "to discuss credit policy and debt management programs which would assist in the highly important fight against inflation and improve public confidence in the market for Government securities", and suggesting a program as the basis for such a discussion. This letter was handed to and discussed with the Secretary of the

Treasury by the Chairman and Vice Chairman of the Federal Open Market Committee. (At this meeting, for the first time, Mr. William McC. Martin, Assistant Secretary of the Treasury, took part in the discussion.)

The matters at issue were now back on the track of responsible discussion by the two agencies of Government whose overlapping responsibilities had erupted into controversy, although there were still a few detours to be traversed. Before the proposed discussions could begin, the Secretary of the Treasury had to enter a hospital to recuperate from an operation and the Treasury sought a commitment from the Open Market Committee that there would be no change in the existing situation in the Government securities market during the period of his hospitalization. This was a commitment which the Committee felt unable to give in the face of mounting inflationary pressures, and a Government securities market which was demanding heavy purchases by the Federal Reserve, contrary to the policy and program which it thought the economic situation required. The Committee asked the Secretary to name someone at the Treasury with whom it could talk, in the interim, and the Secretary named Mr. Martin.

Negotiations now took a turn for the better. Mr. Martin suggested that members of the staff of the Treasury Department and of the Federal Reserve meet as soon as possible to go over the proposals contained in the February 7 letter of the Federal Open Market Committee to the Secretary of the Treasury, and such other ideas as might be brought forward. (Chairman McCabe had previously suggested such staff conferences, but the Secretary of the Treasury had said he preferred to settle matters at the policy level and then have the details worked out at staff levels.) A working party was created[4] and progress began to be made toward understanding at the "technical level" for referral to the "policy level", as the Treasury phrased it, although the negotiation faltered at times.

[4] Mr. Martin, Mr. George Haas, Director of Technical Research, and Mr. Edward Bartelt, Fiscal Assistant Secretary, from the Treasury, and Mr. Winfield Riefler, Assistant to the Chairman of the Board of Governors and Secretary of the Federal Open Market Committee, Mr. Woodlief Thomas, economist of the Committee, and Mr. Robert Rouse, Manager of the System Open Market Account and Vice President of the Federal Reserve Bank of New York.

While these discussions were going on, the White House again intervened. A meeting was called by the President on February 26, 1951, including the Director of Defense Mobilization, the Under Secretary of the Treasury (in the absence of the Secretary), the Assistant Secretary of the Treasury (Mr. Martin), the Chairman of the Securities and Exchange Commission, the Chairman and Vice Chairman of the Federal Open Market Committee, the members of the Council of Economic Advisers and the special counsel of the President. At this meeting the President began by reading a memorandum (which was also released to the press), in which he expressed his concern with the problem of reconciling the need to maintain stability in the Government securities market and the need to restrain credit expansion; outlined the general economic program of the Administration; and requested the Secretary of the Treasury, the Chairman of the Federal Reserve Board, the Director of Defense Mobilization, and the Chairman of the Council of Economic Advisers to study the problem of the overlapping responsibilities of the Treasury and the Federal Reserve System. He also expressed the hope that "while this study is under way, no attempt will be made to change the interest rate pattern, so that stability in the Government securities market will be maintained". This intervention was different in form from previous interventions and came more nearly to grips with the problem, but it also failed to recognize that the Federal Reserve has duties laid upon it by the Congress which cannot be abandoned to the arbitration of *ad hoc* committees. Fortunately, the Treasury-Federal Reserve "Accord" was reached while the Presidential committee was still pondering the problem, and when its report was later completed it apparently was "filed".

The tenor of informed thinking in the Congress, which was the only place the dispute could be decided, in default of agreement by the two agencies directly involved, was indicated in a powerful speech by Senator Douglas in the Senate chamber on February 22, 1951, which he concluded with a plea "that the Treasury abate its policies and yield on this issue" and that "the Federal Reserve gird its legal loins and fulfill the responsibilities which I believe the Congress intended it to have".

Meanwhile, the negotiations of the principals in the dispute regained their momentum. On February 28, the staff negotiators felt that matters were sufficiently well in hand to warrant presentation to their principals and, that evening, the Secretary of the Treasury was consulted by Mr. Martin and the request was made by the Secretary that Mr. Martin and Mr. Bartelt be permitted, orally, to present to the Federal Open Market Committee the response of the Treasury to the Committee letter of February 7, 1951. Consideration of this report by the Committee evoked a generally favorable response, and the staff group of the Committee was requested to resume its discussion with the Treasury group, in the light of the views expressed by the members of the Committee.

The Federal Open Market Committee met again on March 2, and Mr. Riefler reported the results of the final staff conference with the Treasury representatives. There ensued a further discussion of all the points on which agreement was being sought, and a concise statement of a program acceptable to the Open Market Committee was written and given to Messrs. Martin and Bartelt for their consideration, and later discussed with them at length by Messrs. McCabe, Sproul, Riefler, and Thomas. A meeting of minds was achieved along the following lines:

1. Purpose—to reduce to a minimum the creation of bank reserves through monetization of the public debt, while assuring the financing of the Government's needs.

2. A conversion offering by the Treasury which would be designed to remove a substantial amount of the long-term restricted[5] 2½ percent bonds from the market.

3. Support of the market for the outstanding restricted 2½ percent bonds by the Federal Open Market Committee at par or slightly above for a limited amount and only during the brief period of the conversion offering.

4. With the exception of this support, the maintenance of orderly market conditions, hereafter,

[5] *I.e.*, purchase restricted to noncommercial bank investors.

to be without reference to the maintenance of the par value of any Treasury issues.

5. Reduction or discontinuance of purchases of short-term Government securities by the System Open Market Account, so as to permit yields on such securities to fluctuate around the discount rate (1¾ percent) and thus to make that rate effective, with the understanding that it would not be changed during the remainder of the year, except in compelling circumstances.

6. Prior consultation between the Treasury and Federal Reserve on changes in debt management or credit policy, unless extraordinary circumstances made such prior consultation impossible.

7. The public statement of agreement to be brief, financial, and nonpolitical.

The terms of agreement were taken by Mr. Martin to the Secretary of the Treasury, at the hospital, and the program was cleared with him and then with the members of the Federal Open Market Committee on March 3, 1951. The following statement and announcement appeared in the press on Sunday, March 4, 1951:

> *Joint announcement by the Secretary of the Treasury and the Chairman of the Board of Governors and of the Federal Open Market Committee of the Federal Reserve System.*
>
> *The Treasury and the Federal Reserve System have reached full accord with respect to debt management and monetary policies to be pursued in furthering their common purpose to assure the successful financing of the Government's requirements and, at the same time, to minimize monetization of the public debt.*

Simultaneously, the Secretary of the Treasury announced that there would be an offering for a limited period of a new investment series of long-term nonmarketable Treasury bonds in exchange for the two longest outstanding restricted Treasury bonds (the 2½ percent bonds of June and December 1967-72). The details of this offering were announced March 19. The offering was a 2¾ percent bond of 1975-80 which, while nonmarketable, could be converted at the holder's option into five-year marketable notes carrying a coupon of 1½ percent. More than two thirds ($13.6 billion) of the outstanding 2½ percent bonds of 1967-72 were turned in for the new 2¾ percent bonds in this first offering. (A year later another $1.8 billion of the new bonds was issued in exchange for the four longest issues of outstanding restricted bonds.)

During the transition period, over the next six weeks, the System Open Market Account and some of the Treasury investment accounts purchased substantial amounts of long-term Treasury bonds at declining prices, in order to ease the adjustment in the market to the final abandonment of the "pattern of rates" and its long-term anchor of 2½ percent. By April 12, 1951 the initial price adjustments were completed and the market "bottomed out". Happily, the inflationary pressures which had brought matters to a head between the Treasury and the Federal Reserve subsided after the first quarter of 1951, and for this the release of monetary policy from the shackles of a "pattern of rates" received a modicum of credit.

If it is too much to say that the Treasury and the Federal Reserve have lived happily ever after the "Accord", they at least have learned to get along together with a minimum of marital friction.

There could be discord again, of course, but it is less likely if the experience and lessons of the "Accord" period are remembered. As a contribution to this remembrance, here are some gleanings.

1. In situations and areas where debt management and credit policy overlap, neither the Treasury nor the Federal Reserve System should make final decisions without responsive consultation and without due regard for the responsibilities and views of its partner.

2. Continuous communication provides the basis for such sharing of responsibility. In the pre-"Accord" period there was a failure of communication which helped to lead to the breaking of this rule. The Federal Reserve thought it understood the position of the Treasury, but it may not have. There is good reason to believe that the Treasury did not understand the posi-

tion of the Federal Reserve. For the latter lack of understanding, the Federal Reserve bore some blame. Although its basic objective was to regain the initiative with respect to the creation of bank reserves, much of its argument with the Treasury was couched in terms of interest rates. The interest rate structure, of course, was the place where Federal Reserve policy would directly and obviously impinge on debt management, but concentration on small changes in interest rates tended to reduce discussion to a question of "hat sizes" in the minds of the Treasury and, to some extent, of the Congress and the public. The Federal Reserve had come to believe, however, that with a greatly enlarged Federal debt and a nearly homogeneous national money market, an opportunity had been created for effective action with limited variation in interest rates and that, for the time being, its objectives could be achieved by restoring modest rate flexibility at the short end of the rate structure.

3. In the absence of understanding and acceptance of this belief, the Treasury viewed with some doubt the strength of purpose of the Federal Reserve to maintain the $2\frac{1}{2}$ percent rate on outstanding long-term Treasury bonds, since the maintenance of this ceiling on the rate structure limited the permissible variation of rates lower down the maturity schedule. The Federal Reserve was aware of this restriction, but was willing to accept it for a time because of its belief that there would need to be an extensive shifting in the portfolios of investing institutions out of long-term Government securities and into corporate bonds, mortgages, and other debt instruments of the private sector of the economy in the reconversion period, and that this shift would have to be eased along if serious market unsettlement was to be avoided. In performing this orderly market service, the Federal Reserve tried to offset the effect of its bond purchases on bank reserves by selling equivalent amounts of short-term Government securities, and had considerable success. Continued success in this maneuver, however, needed the assistance of higher interest rates on the short-term securities being sold.

4. Finally, in the catalogue of misunderstanding, there was the general Treasury opinion that the credit program which the Federal Reserve wished to follow would be of little use in combating inflationary pressures, particularly in the Korean period, and that "experimenting" with the interest rate structure could weaken faith in the Government securities market and in the credit of the Government at a time when major war financing might be necessary. The Federal Reserve, on the contrary, believed that faith in Government credit and confidence in Government securities would be destroyed if it became apparent that monetary policy was to be prevented from fighting inflationary pressures and that a dollar invested in Government securities would be a shrunken dollar when the securities matured.

Up to the time of the Korean crisis, the Federal Reserve was content to carry on a holding operation. It joined with the Treasury in opposing those who, in the immediate postwar years, counseled abrupt and vigorous use of credit policy to reduce the swollen money supply, inherited from the war, and to wring excess liquidity out of the economy. Rather, it took the position that the economy would have to grow up to the money supply (which it rapidly did) and that, meanwhile, release of inflationary pressures suppressed by direct control during the war period would be partially offset by increases in the national product (as they were). In the face of the economic repercussions of the Korean crisis, however, such an approach was no longer practical.

5. The Korean confrontation focused attention on the core of the problem. Coequal Government agencies, with certain overlapping responsibilities, had been unable to arrive at a common policy other than by the subordination of one agency to the other. Various answers to this problem were suggested.

(a) A clearer Congressional mandate. There is no clear mandate to the Treasury with respect to the broader economic implications of debt management and no clear mandate to the Federal Reserve System with respect to the maintenance of price stability and the international position of the dollar. As mentioned earlier, a subcommittee of the Joint Economic Committee—in 1950—recommended that it be expressed as the will of the Congress that transactions with respect to money and credit and transactions in the Federal debt be made consistent with the policies of the Federal Reserve. This recommendation followed the dictum of Senator Douglas that "good fences make good neighbors", but when the location of the property line is uncertain and the line may change at times, "good fences" are not an adequate answer.

Both the Treasury and the Federal Reserve have affirmed that, in addition to Congressional directives applying to them specifically, they consider themselves bound by the declaration of policy set forth in the Employment Act of 1946. What remains to be done, in terms of a Congressional mandate to the Federal Reserve System, it seems to me, is to include a reference to price stability among the general guides to economic well-being in the preamble of the Employment Act, and to add a general directive with respect to price stability and the international position of the dollar to the Federal Reserve Act.

This will not satisfy those who believe that a central bank should pursue a primary objective—stable purchasing power of the monetary unit—without being diverted by a wider range of economic objectives such as are set forth in the Employment Act of 1946. Certainly the Federal Reserve System must have its own objectives in the field of monetary policy and realize its capacities and limitations, but I do not believe that it is possible in the light of the Employment Act, and what it reflects of national purpose, for the central bank to be completely free.

(b) Another suggestion for resolving conflicts of the Treasury and Federal Reserve, where their interest and duties overlap, and which usually draws considerable support, is the establishment of an interagency consultative committee or a national monetary and credit council, which would bring together the heads of a number of Government agencies having responsibilities related to credit policy and debt management. This would be expected to provide for informal collaboration, although the body would be without directive powers, which most agree would be an usurpation of Congressional authority. This sort of thing sounds good in conversation and looks good on paper, but the only people who can resolve differences arising out of overlapping statutory responsibilities are people who bear the responsibility and know what it is all about—that is, the people at the Treasury and in the Federal Reserve System in this case. A committee or council of the sort proposed either languishes on the vine because of a lack of authority, or becomes a means of exerting executive pressure on a body (the Federal Reserve) which draws its powers from the Congress.

(c) There are some who think, of course, that the Federal Reserve System should be made more responsive to the Executive Branch of the Government and, presumably, that the President by virtue of his office or the power of his presence should be able to order a composition of contrary views held by Treasury and Federal Reserve officials. Whether as a three-man body, with the President holding the balance between Treasury and Federal Reserve, or as a council made up, on one side, of a number of individuals holding Presidential appointments and owing Presidential loyalty as a part of a political administration and, on the other side, by a representative of the Federal Reserve System, this kind of proposal has little to recommend it. In the words of a witness (Beardsley Ruml, formerly Chairman of the Board of the Federal Reserve Bank of New York) at the hearing of the Patman subcommittee of the Joint Committee on the Economic Report in 1952, bringing the President in to settle differences between the Federal Reserve and the Treasury would mean that one or both parties to the disagreement would devote their efforts to procuring a favorable opinion from the President, and would lead to the use of force rather than reason in dealing with an agency of the Congress which has statutory duties. "Nothing but harm to public confidence in both money and Government would result."

This is not to say that the Chairman of the Board of Governors should not discuss the problems of the Federal Reserve System with the President, alone or with the Secretary of the Treasury. That is natural and, at times, desirable. But to make this a regular means of coordination of policies can lead to dictation instead of persuasion, as the experience of the pre-"Accord" period attests.

(d) Then there are those who would substitute an invariable formula for fallible human judgment or weak human resolve in directing monetary affairs and, so long as the Federal Reserve followed the formula (if it retained its job at all), the Treasury (and everyone else) would have to accommodate its objectives to the working of the formula. Ideally, one exponent of this theory says[6] "the surest way to achieve the aim of a stable monetary structure is. . .to legislate a rule specifying the behavior of the quantity of money. The rule I favor is one which specifies that the quantity of money shall grow at a steady rate from week to week, month to month, and year to year". But when this invariable formula is related to an existing and future state of affairs, and when account is taken of the lag between monetary action and its economic effects, he says that "the problem of lag in reaction and the fact that the effects are spread over a period is not a problem that can be solved by just looking at the quantity of money. In order to solve that problem or in order to eliminate that difficulty it would be necessary to forecast what is going to happen much better than we now can." So, in point of fact, except as an assertion that an invariable formula would have made fewer mistakes than have been made without such a formula, he says we do

[6] Professor Milton Friedman at the hearings on "The Federal Reserve System after Fifty Years", held by the Subcommittee on Domestic Finance of the Committee on Banking and Currency, House of Representatives, March 3, 1964.

not "know enough now to set up a formula . . .which would do more good than harm". I am willing to wait, at least until we have more persuasive arguments that a rigid invariable formula can ride through the continuing changes in the economic environment, without the benefit of human judgment and without causing major errors instead of minor ones.

My own conclusion is that the experience of the "Accord" leads to a more human and natural solution of the problem of the overlapping responsibilities of the Treasury and the Federal Reserve than any of the corrective devices which have been suggested. It is the solution which has been working since the "Accord". It involves the recognition that Treasury and the Federal Reserve are coequals in the area of their overlapping responsibilities. It is based on the assumption that informed and responsible men recognize that, in our form of Government, such sharing of responsibility requires thorough discussion of divergent views and every effort to merge them into a common purpose. It demands that there be open and frequent communication between those who determine policy, that the makers of policy have staffs of the highest competence which also are in open and frequent communication, and that the policymakers have a sufficient understanding of the theory and practice of their art to be able to add wisdom to knowledge when positions show signs of becoming unyielding. Finally, it assumes that the Congress, presumably through the Joint Economic Committee on the Economic Report, will continue to monitor performance and to provide evidence of the attitude of the Congress toward performance because, if irreconcilable differences do arise, the Congress must be the final arbiter in matters concerning the power to regulate the "people's money".

The Federal Reserve challenge to the Treasury's assertion of dominance in the area of their overlapping responsibilities prior to the "Accord" had its ultimate justification in the achievement of coequal status in these matters, and not as an assertion of a false independence. The Federal Reserve does not have, never has had, and never has claimed to have an independence in monetary affairs which divorces it from the general economic policies of the Government.

Letter to Robert T. Stevens

August 28, 1950

Mr. Robert T. Stevens
Chairman, Board of Directors
Federal Reserve Bank of New York

Dear Bob:

Your letter of August 24 reminds me that I had a vacation. I had almost forgotten it.

I returned to New York in time to attend the directors' meeting on August 17, and then went to Washington for a meeting of the Federal Open Market Committee on Friday, the 18th. At that meeting I was in the chair most of the day as Tom was fogbound between Northeast Harbor, Maine, and Washington. It was the view of the Committee, which I must admit I steered in that direction, that inflationary pressures were strong and increasing, that announced Government policy is to restrain these pressures by fiscal and credit measures rather than by all-out direct controls, and that it was high time we did something to restrain the rapid expansion of bank credit. We knew, of course, that legislation was in the works to fix controls over mortgage credit and consumer credit—two sore spots—but we also knew that it would take time to pass this legislation and time to set up its administration. In addition, we felt that selective controls would not be enough in any case, that bank credit of all sorts was expanding, and that general credit controls should be used. We decided, therefore, to act in our sphere of primary responsibility, the control of credit, by refusing to provide further reserves to the banking system at existing rates. We also decided to tell the Treasury what we had done, rather than to formulate our action in terms of a recommendation to the Treasury as to the rates it should place on its September-October refundings, its action in its primary sphere of responsibility. The fact that these two spheres of responsibility are the opposite sides of the same coin is what causes the difficulty.

Tom was in agreement with all this when he joined the meeting, and he and I saw the Secretary that afternoon and told him what we had decided to do and why, both with respect to the New York Bank discount rate and open market operations. The Secretary was brief and abrupt, indicating that since we had told him what we had decided to do there was nothing for him to say. Tom asked him if he agreed with us, and he again said there was nothing for him to say. I said I did not think we should ask his blessing—that we should take sole responsibility for our action—but we could hope for his acquiescence and, perhaps, his later approval if our action worked out well. We then told him we had a statement for the press in preparation which we had hoped would reach him before we left his office, and that we would telephone it to him as soon as it was ready.

Tom and I returned to the Board building and in a few minutes a call came through from the Secretary. He told Tom that he was announcing his September-October financing immediately and that it was 13-month 1¼s for all maturities, totaling $13 billion plus. This was contrary to all the advice he had received from any source I know of; and, of course, ran directly counter to our program. Tom read him our statement and pointed out the conflict, but the Secretary had made up his mind. This is the way, on two recent occasions (last winter and late this spring), he had throttled us by early announcements of forthcoming refundings. This time we had decided we must stick to our course, even though he again tried this maneuver.

The result is a messy situation both in terms of our relations with the Treasury and with the market, and in terms of our broad objective. We are trying to implement what we understand to be Government policy by trying to restrain excessive expansion of bank credit, as a holding action, until the stronger weapon of higher taxes can be brought into play in the battle to control inflation. At the same time, we cannot permit a large Treasury refunding to fail completely, particularly in time of war. As a consequence, we are buying very large amounts of the September-October maturities at par to protect the Treasury's refunding, while letting the yields in the rest of the market rise above a rate of 1¼ percent for one year. Obviously, few will want to exchange their maturing holdings for 13-month 1¼s when they can buy shorter maturities at higher yields or improve their earnings position by buying longer maturities. To offset our purchases of the maturing issues, we are allowing some of our bill maturities to mature without replacement and selling other securities as and when we can at the higher yields which have developed.

A large part of the public reaction to all this has been, of course, that it is a flare-up of an old fight between the Treasury and the Federal Reserve. That makes the most striking news story. The public attitude on that may well be that "We don't know who is right, but this is no time to be fighting among ourselves". It is important, therefore, that we make it clear as and when we can (without engaging in a battle of statements with the Secretary) that there is more to this than a clash of personalities or agencies on the question of whether short-term rates should be an eighth or a quarter higher or lower. The fundamentals are two:

(1) Is inflation in the present circumstances going to be controlled by adequate credit and fiscal measures or are we going to let it go, perhaps later moving into direct controls?

(2) Are we going to have a central banking system which has some power and authority with respect to interest rates, within the terms of general Government policy, or is this no longer possible in view of the Treasury's debt management problems and the Government's debt position?

The Congress may have to render the decision on these points, and an informed public opinion will be most important. I think that, if we can make it clear that confidence in the credit of the Government and in the dollar can be preserved, not by freezing interest rates and prices, but by giving evidence of a will to restrain inflation, we can win. There is a growing feeling that Government securities are a poor investment because the dollar you get back isn't the same dollar you put in, and there is a dangerous chance that people might begin to change dollars for "things" if they become convinced that another substantial rise in prices of "things" is inevitable.

So far as the New York Bank's discount rate is concerned, I was not distressed by it as I recognized that the tide was running strongly for action when I left on vacation. As it turned out, it was fortunate that we were ready with a higher discount rate at the time of the Open Market Committee meeting, a week ago Friday. This gave the Board of Governors something specific on which to act immediately, and gave us a peg on which to hang our public statement. There are difficulties about making a public statement with respect to specific open market operations, because you may tip your hand before you are ready. Our directors were a little impatient, I think, but in the end their action fitted in very nicely.

I hope you are having a fine vacation and will be ready for anything when you return on September 7. It will be good to have you back.

With best regards,

Yours sincerely,

Allan

Letter to C.F. Cobbold

September 18, 1950

Mr. C.F. Cobbold
Governor, Bank of England

My dear Cobbold:

I find I am a little behind in my correspondence as a result of a holiday in California (which I enjoyed thoroughly), and the events which began to take shape as soon as I returned to the Bank at mid-August.

First, with regard to our studies of the general balance-of-payments position and particularly with reference to your letter of July 20, the Korean situation and the rearmament program of the Western world have obviously made all previous estimates and hopes out of date. Presently I don't think we can foresee what deterioration in previous trade expectations may develop, over time. Nor can we see what the balance-of-payments effects of the rearmament program may be. The only thing that emerges clearly, so far as I am concerned, is that some form of mutual aid will be necessary after 1952 and that, while hope is deferred, we can nevertheless keep our ultimate objectives in mind.

I am not surprised that you are bewildered by the position in this market. It really is an old story, however, and one with which you are familiar. It seemed to us in the Federal Reserve System, and to most others in Government and out, that inflationary pressures were building up and that whatever steps could be taken to damp them down should be taken. The Government, both in its executive and legislative branches, decided that reliance in this effort would be placed, at least for the present, on fiscal and credit measures. Direct controls were not to be used, at least for the present, except in special circumstances. There was, therefore, no attempt at central bank defiance of Government policy, as we understood it, in what we have done. We felt, rather, that our continuing responsibility to promote stable progress in the economy had been given an added weight. We knew, of course, that increased taxes were in process of enactment and we believe this to be the country's main reliance. We also knew that powers of selective control of credit—instalment credit and mortgage credit—were in the works and that these would be helpful, since much loose lending was going on in these areas. We could not, however, ignore the excessive expansion of bank credit in other fields and this called for general credit controls, however modest.

In the circumstances, instead of trying to recommend to the Treasury what term and rate it should put on its September and October refundings, which obviously is primarily its responsibility, we advised the Treasury of what we were going to do to make it a little more difficult and a little more costly for the banks to get additional reserve funds, which is primarily our responsibility. Since these powers and responsibilities overlap, or are the reverse sides of the same coin, one would hope for agreed and coordinated action. This we had sought, in one circumstance or another, over many months, with meager results. This time we went our separate way and the Treasury went its way.

The result was a rise in short-term rates which made the Treasury's offering of $13½ billion of 13-month 1¼ percent notes (in exchange for maturities of 2½ percent bonds, 2 percent bonds, and 1 ⅛ percent notes called or due September 15 and October 1) largely unacceptable to the market. We then set ourselves to buy as much of the maturing issues as we could so that the Treasury might not have a complete failure in these difficult times, and to sell as much of our existing holdings as we could, so that we would not be forced to put funds into the market, contrary to our avowed objective. The result was Alice in Wonderland in some ways, but we have been able to come out fairly well so far. The Treasury got its money, or most of it, at 1¼ percent, short-term rates have gone up to about 1⅜ percent for one year, and the money market has been on the "tight" side much of the time.

This sort of thing can't go on. Maybe minds will be clearer and agreement more likely as a result of what has happened, or maybe anger or resentment will prevent calm consideration. I don't know. The Treasury doesn't believe that small changes in interest rates can have any effect on strong inflationary pressures, such as we are now exposed to, and no one thinks of drastic action such as might have been taken in "olden days". On the other hand, it is quite sensitive about increases in the cost of servicing the debt. We shall have to try again to work out a coordinated program. Failing that, the Congress might have to take a hand in deciding how our overlapping authorities and responsibilities are to be exercised. This matter was discussed last December and commented upon in the report of hearings of the Douglas Subcommittee of the Congressional Joint Committee on the Economic Report. Despite the encouragement of this report, experience would suggest that the odds are against us, but time and circumstance could be in our favor. In any case, we had a present responsibility we felt we must meet.

With best regards,

Yours sincerely,

Allan Sproul

Letter to Thomas B. McCabe

February 20, 1951

Mr. Thomas B. McCabe
Chairman, Board of Governors
Federal Reserve System

Dear Tom:

At the meeting of the Executive Committee of the Board of Directors of this bank on February 8 (at which I was not present because I was attending a meeting of the Federal Open Market Committee at Washington), and again at a meeting of the Committee on February 15, there was extended discussion of credit policy and debt management, of the differences which have developed and persisted between the Treasury and the Federal Reserve System, and of the responsibilities of the directors in the circumstances. It was the consensus of the directors present that positive action should now be taken by the System to restrain the further expansion of bank credit, and that they, as directors, had perhaps been remiss in not urging more vigorous action, during the past several months, while inflationary pressures have been mounting.

At the same time, the directors find themselves somewhat at a loss in defending the Federal Reserve System and in promoting its policies, in the absence of definitive word from the Board of Governors and the Federal Open Market Committee as to what their policy is, whether support of policy within the System is unanimous or divided, and whether the policy will be pursued over Treasury opposition or not.

I have told the directors, in the past, of my own personal views and I have now told them what I could of our present situation and about the efforts we are again making to reach an accommodation with the Treasury, short of abandoning those policies which we think are essential to help prevent further inflation and consequent loss of confidence in the credit of the Government and in the dollar. The difficulties of making a clarifying public statement in these circumstances were recognized, but the idea that such a statement is not desirable was reluctantly accepted, if at all.

On the basis of these discussions, I am sure that the directors strongly support the kind of program we have in mind, which is to deprive the banks of further ready access to reserve funds, assuming the possible risks of the rise in short-term rates and the decline in prices of long-term bonds which would follow. They would urge us only to put the program into effect as promptly as possible, doing what we think is right in terms of our statutory responsibilities and the present economic situation. I think they would want us to do this regardless of Treasury opposition, if that continues, leaving to the Congress the final determination as to whether or not we have performed our duties faithfully and well.

Because they feel this strongly, and because they believe that you and your fellow members of the Board of Governors have a right to know their views, they have asked me to write you in this vein.

Yours faithfully,

Allan Sproul

Letter to James E. Shelton

February 28, 1951

Mr. James E. Shelton
President, American Bankers Association
c/o Security-First National Bank
Los Angeles, California

Dear Jim:

I see that you are going to speak at the Annual Savings and Mortgage Conference of the A.B.A., here in New York on March 5. Your subject is listed in the program as "1951 — A Critical Year".

It is almost certainly going to be a critical year for the Federal Reserve System and for the whole banking system. It looks as if there is going to have to be a determination, probably by the Congress, as to whether we are to have a central banking system, such as we thought we had, or whether it is to become, in essence, a bureau of the Treasury; whether we are going to be able to have a credit policy somewhat divorced from the stark needs of Treasury borrowing and unilateral decisions as to debt management, which directly and indirectly involve credit policy. This is a great banking issue, and I would be sorry to see you ignore it during your term of office as President of the American Bankers Association.

Please do not let anyone tell you that all this commotion is just so much buildup by the Board of Governors preparatory to another "grab for power" over reserves of the member banks. I do not know whether or not the Board of Governors will ask the Congress for additional powers over member bank reserves, nor whether the Treasury will support such a request, but that isn't the main issue. The main issue is whether credit policy is to make its contribution—now—to restraint of the tremendous inflationary pressures in the economy. We are completely serious about the need to curb any further expansion of bank reserves, through open market operations and the discount rate, and I should think you would be equally serious about curbing any further aggregate expansion of bank credit. We can't do our job if we have to support Government securities at their present levels or at any fixed level, and 14,000 individual banks, even with a voluntary agreement, can't do their job if we don't do ours given the competitive situation which exists. The Treasury has demanded, in effect, that we give fixed support to the Government securities market at present levels as part of what it calls financial mobilization for defense. That means the abandonment of all control over bank reserves, as was the case during the war, and it helps to expose the country to another round of dollar debasement such as we inherited from our war finance. I should think the banks of the country would want us to use all our powers to help prevent such a tragic encore, since under present circumstances it can be done without risk to the defense program, full production, and employment, and since it should contribute to greater confidence in the credit of the Government, which means the dollar, rather than the reverse.

That is why I was sorry to see you spend so much time in a recent talk berating the idea of increased Board powers over reserve requirements, and raising the cry of socialism, while consigning to the fine print your remarks on what I consider to be the real issue. I don't care much whether you, or the A.B.A., are for or against increased powers over reserve requirements, so long as you take a stand in favor of effective action to combat inflation, including action to curb further expansion of bank credit and the money supply which feed the inflationary fires. I care mightily whether you, the A.B.A., and the many fine bankers of the country really discuss the issues involved in the controversy between the Federal Reserve System and the Treasury and reach objective conclusions. I continue to hope that you will promote such discussion, so that if and when the issue comes before the Congress the bankers of the country will not be unprepared to take a stand on principle, rather than on expediency and temporary political advantage. This is not an argument about eighths or thirty-seconds. It is an argument about a fundamental question of economic and financial policy.

If you have any time when you are in New York, I should be glad to talk with you about all this.

Yours faithfully,

Allan Sproul
President

P.S. I haven't mentioned the more arbitrary controls over bank lending, which some are suggesting, as a way to restrict credit and peg interest rates at the same time. I assume we would all abhor this kind of Government control. If you are afraid of state socialism, this would be it.

Letter to Murray J. Rossant
New York Times

February 10, 1963

Dear Murray:

The trial balloons having been launched and having floated quite well, the reappointment of Bill Martin has now been made official. He can leave whenever he wants, with colors flying, which is as it should be. Meanwhile, as a symbol of the monetary conscience of the administration, he is useful at home and abroad and, to paraphrase his favorite phrase, he can lean with as well as against the wind.

In the preliminary stories concerning the president's intentions, however, there was one historical note to which, as a member of the society against creating history by constant repetition, I take exception. The Western edition of the *Times* for February 6, in a brief sketch of Bill Martin's career, said that "In the 'Accord' drafted primarily by Mr. Martin and Winfield Riefler of the Board's staff, the pegging was discontinued." The "Accord" was not drafted primarily by Martin and Riefler. The general basis for the "Accord" was laid down by the Federal Open Market Committee, itself, in a letter from the then chairman of the Committee to the then Secretary of the Treasury early in February 1951.

The terms of the specific program, which became the "Accord", were set forth in a statement prepared by the Federal Open Market Committee, in meeting assembled, and subsequently handed to the waiting representatives of the Secretary of the Treasury. In between these events, the Secretary had gone to the hospital, and had appointed Mr. Martin and two associates at the Treasury to carry on exploratory conversations "at the technical level" with representatives of the FOMC.

The "Accord" was only an accord by courtesy. Actually, it was almost entirely a statement by the Federal Open Market Committee of what it was prepared to do and not to do in the related fields of monetary policy and debt management, so as to free itself of any obligation to support fixed prices of Government securities. The unique feature of the program was the offering of a long-term nonmarketable 2¾ percent bond in exchange for outstanding 2½ percent bonds of 1967-72, with a provision for conversion of the nonmarketable bonds into marketable five-year 1½ percent notes. This was a proposal advanced by Mr. Riefler. It provided a bridge over which the Treasury could retreat from its insistence on the maintenance of a ceiling rate of 2½ percent for Treasury bonds. At the same time, it offered a means of removing from the market a large amount of 2½ percent bonds which the holders were pressing for sale so that they might invest their funds in higher yielding obligations.

Mr. Martin's contribution to the "Accord", I think, was to get the Secretary of the Treasury to accede to the terms laid down by the Federal Open Market Committee, as the best way out of a bad situation.

As they say, I wanted you to have this bit of lore, in case anything happens to me.

Sincerely,

Allan Sproul

Letter to Murray J. Rossant
New York Times

September 3, 1966

Dear Murray:

I see that former President Truman has gotten into the act. His concern is proper, although his reasoning leaves something to be desired and his recollections are faulty. As one who has entered the age of reminiscence, my attention was drawn to the latter aspect of what he said.

The "threats" from the Federal Reserve during the latter part of his administration, to which he refers, were really threats against the Federal Reserve coming from his office, his advisers, and the Treasury. The "Government prevailed", as he claims, in the sense that the Federal Reserve had the backing of strong Congressional opinion and refused dictation from the President. The System even had to give out a statement (by Marriner Eccles) saying that a report of our meeting with the President, given out by his office and the Treasury, was incorrect. Or, as he would say, false. Your editorial on his statement was easy on him, as it should have been. After all, he was President of the United States, he is in his eighties, and he never did know anything about economics.

I am going to attend the Bank and Fund meetings at Washington at the end of the month, an invitation from George Woods having overcome my resolution of about fifteen years' standing to forego these mass celebrations. After the meetings I shall be in New York for a couple of weeks and I shall hope to see you.

Sincerely,

Allan

Chapter 4

Human Judgment and Central Banking

Aside from the need to do something about inflation, no subject was dearer to Sproul's heart than what he viewed as the closely related need to exercise human judgment, however fallible, in the conduct of monetary policy. He rarely let an opportunity go by without calling attention to one or the other, more likely both.

The first of his papers reprinted in the present chapter, "Policy Norms and Central Banking", is the most complete treatment of the "bills only" or "bills preferably" controversy he ever published. It was this conflict, of course, that eventually led to his departure from the Federal Reserve System. He went about writing the paper with his usual historical thoroughness: starting with 1880 and putting "bills only" in the context in which he had always visualized it—as a particular instance of the eternal search for a mechanical rule to replace human judgment and discretion in economic policymaking.

"Practicing central bankers (and the governments to which they are responsible)", he concluded, "cannot afford to be confined by formulae which attempt to cope, in precise measure, with the actions and anticipations of millions of human beings exercising a high degree of economic freedom of choice. Monetary policy can continue to make its contribution to the goals of vigorous sustainable economic growth, maximum attainable production and employment, and reasonable stability of prices, if its practitioners continue to sharpen their analyses of complex economic developments and continue to base their actions upon a balanced view of total situations. They cannot be relieved of this difficult task by doctrinaire policy norms."

This article is followed, in the present chapter, by his historic 1954 Congressional testimony on "bills only", when he opposed Chairman Martin head-on before the Subcommittee on Economic Stabilization of the Joint Economic Committee (then known as the Joint Committee on the Economic Report). It was not an easy task for a long-time organization man, and he could hardly avoid frequent misgivings.

Three 1961 letters and a 1963 address at New York University conclude the chapter. The first two of the letters (to Murray Rossant and Alfred Hayes) are replies to communications received shortly after the Federal Open Market Committee abandoned "bills only" in February 1961.

The third letter, to Henry Alexander, Chairman of the Board of Morgan Guaranty Trust Company, was written and mailed from Zurich, Switzerland. A day before the Sprouls were to leave on a three-month trip to Europe, Mr. Alexander had handed him a copy of the April 1961 issue of the Morgan Guaranty *Survey,* containing an article entitled "A Closer Look at Interest Rate Relationships". The article attempted to show by various statistical techniques that there is a high degree of covariation between short-term and long-term interest rates, with minimal time lags, leaving the impression that the abandonment of "bills only" a few weeks earlier by the Open Market Committee had been a mistake.

Although Sproul was on vacation, he found it impossible to postpone a response until his return home. He wrote the letter by hand in Zurich and mailed it to Alexander in that form, although he knew that his handwriting was almost illegible. "I hope you can and will read this", he wrote; "Miss Regan at the Reserve Bank will decipher and type it for you if necessary, I am sure."

From *Men, Money, and Policy,*
Essays in Honor of Karl R. Bopp
Federal Reserve Bank of Philadelphia, 1970

Policy Norms and Central Banking

From the earliest days of central banking in its primitive forms to the present era in which central banks, as the national monetary authorities, are charged with promoting the general economic interests of the nations they serve, domestically and internationally, there has been a continuous pursuit of a will-o'-the-wisp—a policy norm which would guide the operations of such banks with a minimum intrusion of fallible human judgment. The theory has been that a central bank, or any monetary control, must have a supreme norm of reference; that it cannot use more than one norm of reference.[1]

The modern beginnings of this passionate pursuit of an elusive object may be traced to misconceptions which have grown up concerning the operation of the international gold standard during the period 1880 to 1914. Prior to that period, the forerunners of present-day central banks were designed primarily to finance governments or acquired a tinge of public responsibility because of the magnitude of their private banking operations. In the years following 1880, however, most of the principal trading nations of the world had linked their currencies to gold—either they were on a "full" gold standard or a "limping" gold standard or a "gold exchange" standard or some combination of these standards—and the central banks of the financially developed countries had taken primary responsibility for maintaining the international convertibility of their national currencies, directly or indirectly, into gold at a legal parity.

Responsibility for a system of fixed exchange rates necessarily focused attention on international movements of goods and services, capital and credit, and on the rise and fall of the country's international reserves (gold or other legal reserves) which could be used as a buffer to confine fluctua-

---

[1] Unpublished paper of Robert B. Warren, Institute of Advanced Study (Princeton, New Jersey).

tions in the exchange rate within a narrow band around parity. The central bank's response to a fall in the exchange rate and a loss of reserves was usually an increase in its discount rate designed to reverse the movement and, with less uniformity, the response to a rise in the exchange rate and a gain of reserves was a reduction of the discount rate. But the timing and extent of such changes were matters of judgment and their effect on the domestic economy, while secondary to the primary objective, did not always go unattended, particularly in times of loss of public confidence and financial crisis. The whole working of the system depended upon a complex of institutions and techniques and economic conditions, domestic and international, favored by a period of relatively moderate shifts of trade and capital movements around multilateral balance, and fostered by the absence of great wars. To describe the system as an automatic gold standard, hardly touched by human hands, is to misrepresent it.

As the studies of Arthur I. Bloomfield have indicated, "Not only did central banking authorities, so far as can be inferred from their actions, not consistently follow any simple or single rule or criterion of policy, or focus exclusively on considerations of convertibility, but they were constantly called upon to exercise, and did exercise, their judgment in such matters as whether or not to act, the kind and extent of action to take, and the instrument or instruments of policy to use. . . . Discretionary judgment and action were an integral part of central banking before 1914, even if monetary management was not oriented toward maintenance of domestic economic growth and employment and stabilization of prices in the broader modern sense."[2]

The discussion in the United States concerning the creation of a central bank, or a central banking system, during the years before the passage of the Federal Reserve Act in 1913 took place in a period when belief in the automatic character of the international gold standard was little tarnished by later heresies; and gold redeemability at home and internationally was a widely accepted article of faith in this country. Attention was centered on changes in the national monetary system which would correct weaknesses in

[2] *Monetary Policy Under the International Gold Standard, 1880-1914,* published by the Federal Reserve Bank of New York.

the domestic banking structure, but which would not interfere with domestic adjustment to "automatic" international monetary arrangements under the gold standard.

The principal purposes of the Federal Reserve Act in a monetary sense and, aside from matters of bank supervision and the pyramiding of bank reserve funds in New York, were as stated in the preamble to the Act: " . . .to furnish an elastic currency and to afford a means of rediscounting commercial paper." The panic of 1907 had focused attention on these problems. Subsequent studies had pinpointed the difficulty as being inherent in a currency largely in the form of gold certificates and national bank notes and in bank reserve requirements which placed a limit on bank loans and investments more or less regardless of the appropriate and changing needs of the economy.

Although there was little specific reference in the final Federal Reserve Act to the promotion of general economic stability and stability of prices, there was a thread of theory running through the consideration of various drafts of the bill which saw in the legislation a means of automatically controlling the volume of currency and bank loans and investments in a way which it was thought would go far to accomplish these purposes. This theory found expression in the so-called "eligibility" provisions of the Act. The paper which the Federal Reserve Banks could discount or purchase ordinarily had to be, in the terminology of the time, "self-liquidating commercial paper"—that is, it had to be based on short-term agricultural, industrial, or commercial transactions which gave assurance of payment at maturity. This was the kind of paper which the Federal Reserve Banks could pledge as collateral (in addition to gold) for Federal Reserve notes, which were to become the elastic part of the currency, and this was the kind of paper which member banks could present to the Federal Reserve Banks for rediscount in order to acquire additional reserve funds with which to support additions to their existing loans and investments. Since the volume of such paper would rise and fall with the transaction needs of the economy, whether in the form of currency or bank deposits subject to check, excessive increases or decreases of currency circulation and excessive expansion or contraction of bank loans and investment would not occur. Or so it was believed.

This experiment in a species of automatic control of central banking operations did not long survive its inclusion in the Federal Reserve Act. It was first eroded because it proved to be impractical in the day-to-day operations of the Reserve Banks, and then was voided by amendment to the Act (in 1916) which permitted Reserve Banks to make advances to member banks on their promissory notes secured by deposit or pledge of United States Government securities.

This was done partly in preparation for financial needs which might arise if the United States entered the war then raging in Europe, but the permanence of the change was the result of an acquired awareness that the concept of eligibility was unrealistic. As stated by Goldenweiser: "Member banks borrow from the Federal Reserve Banks almost exclusively for the purpose of building up their reserve deposits (with the Reserve Banks) to the necessary (required) level. The banks lend money to such customers (and make such investments) as they choose and meet the currency requirements of their depositors. If, as a net result arising out of all their operations, they find themselves short of reserves, they borrow from the Reserve Banks. . . .There is thus no relationship between the character of the discounted paper and the use to which the funds are put." Furthermore, ". . .the theory disregards the fact that banks can expand at a multiple rate on the basis of Federal Reserve credit; consequently, paper representing the movement of goods to market, when discounted with the Federal Reserve Banks, can become the basis of several times its value in loans of an entirely different character."[3] Self-liquidating commercial paper as an automatic means of controlling the expansion and contraction of bank credit or adjusting the money supply to the productive requirements of the economy was a theoretical and mechanical failure. It provided neither a quantitative nor a qualitative norm of central bank policy.

[3] *American Monetary Policy* (1951), p. 126.

Along this chronological road, the idea that central bank policy should find its normal guide in stability of prices was never far from the surface of discussion. It had been around for a long time, but it received increased attention in the United States following World War I, when there was a sharp increase and then a sharp fall in prices, and when Professor Irving Fisher of Yale became a champion and articulate advocate of a dollar of "invariable purchasing power".

He held that the only unstable unit of measurement in civilized countries was the unit of money, that this was a survival of barbarism, and that it was manifest that an economic system which is largely based on agreements made at one date to pay money at another date would have to find a way to adjust its contracts to changes in the purchasing power of money. (The problem is still with us.) This, he argued, had become possible because a means had been devised for measuring the aberrations of an unstable monetary unit, to wit, a representative index number of prices. And his specific proposal was that the monetary authorities should use such an index number of prices as a guide for adjustments (perhaps every two months) in the weight of the gold content of the dollar so as to keep its purchasing power invariable. If prices tended to rise or fall, the movement would be corrected by "loading" or "unloading" the gold in the dollar.

This idea of a "goods dollar" or a "market basket dollar" or a "compensated dollar", in the form suggested, sounded academic and impractical in a country (or a world) which had become accustomed to the idea (if not the practice) that, if external price levels were unstable, it could not keep both its domestic price level and the exchange rate of its currency stable and that (under whatever form of the gold standard it adhered to) it must put stability of the external exchange ahead of stability of the internal price level.

The idea was opposed on other grounds than those growing out of habit and custom, however. It was argued that (a) no price index, no matter how comprehensive, could include all of the things for which money is spent; (b) that the relation between the volume of credit and the level of prices is not precise and determinable but is indirect and inconstant; (c) that things which do not enter into the price-money relationship, such as an increase or decrease in the efficiency of production and distribution, and changes in quality of product would affect an index of prices; and (d) that the movements of a price index which might be used to trigger monetary counteraction would usually be late, since they would refer to past rises or falls in prices, whereas it would be future price moves which should be counteracted.

Despite its break with gold-standard thinking and the defects of the proposal itself, it had a simple and direct appeal which led to its consideration by the Congress at hearings of the Committee on Banking and Currency at the House of Representatives. The proposal was put forward and was the subject of hearings of the Committee in 1926, that all the powers of the Federal Reserve System should be used to promote stability of the price level.

A principal witness opposing such a statutory instruction to the Federal Reserve System was Governor Benjamin Strong of the Federal Reserve Bank of New York. Governor Strong was aware of and used the various agreements which had been advanced in opposition to legislation that would order the Federal Reserve to use all its powers to stabilize price levels, but the main thrust of his testimony was that there could be no mathematical formula for the administration of Federal Reserve policy or for the regulation of prices. He accepted the view that credit is a major influence on prices and that the promotion of price stability should be a major policy objective of the Federal Reserve, but his views had a broader scope, comprising ideas later finding expression in the Employment Act of 1946. They were that the Government, through its various agencies, has a responsibility for maintaining maximum employment and production and promoting economic growth, and that the objective of credit policy should be to insure that there is sufficient money and credit available to conduct the business of the nation and to finance not only seasonal increases in demand but also the annual normal growth of the economy. He was willing to have the powers of the Federal Reserve System used to promote stability of the price level, but he also recognized that choices and compromises had to be made between various objectives at various times and that, in the end, human judgment has to govern the decisions which are made.

Stability of prices as a norm of central bank policy as a supreme norm of reference did not survive (although the Employment Act of 1946 does include promotion of maximum purchasing power in its policy declaration). Other candidates for that honor have arisen or persisted, however. The doctrine of "bills only" (common name) or "bills preferably" (botanical name) may be placed in this category, not because when viewed as a technique of Federal Reserve open market operations it deserves this prominence, but because its proponents came to place so much stress on the avoidance of price and yield effects of open market operations that they finally asserted (and made it a part of the operating directives of the System Open Market Account) that the sole purpose of open market operations is the provision and absorption of reserves (excepting the correction of disorderly markets in Government securities). This was an attempt to elevate what first had been advanced as a matter of technique to the eminence of a mechanical rule of Federal Reserve policy—a "supreme norm of reference" for the principal element of flexible and effective central bank policy in the United States.

The controversy which this doctrine aroused for several years until it was abandoned in 1961 resulted in a considerable literature and involved emotions which seemed to widen and distort the differences of those who favored and those who opposed the policy. In a broad survey such as this, no extended discussion of all the arguments which were brought forward on both sides can be attempted. Only a summary presentation of its life history from birth to death is possible. The formal birth certificate was recorded in May 1951 when the Federal Open Market Committee voted to authorize its Chairman (William McC. Martin) to appoint a committee to make a study of the Government securities market. But the idea had been conceived earlier by members of the staff of the Board of Governors (and of the Open Market Committee) who not only were interested in the operation of the Government securities market as a channel through which to reach and regulate the reserve position of the member banks, but who also were dissatisfied with the performance of the management of the System Open Market Account at the Federal Reserve Bank of New York and with the power distribution involved in the linkage between policymaking by the Federal Open Market Committee at Washington and the execution of policy by the New York Bank. The study committee, which became known as the Ad Hoc Subcommittee, was set up and began its work in May 1952, and its findings and recommendations became a subject of discussion at a meeting of the Federal Open Market Committee in March 1953, after a delay which was reported to have stemmed from the fact that it had become apparent that "the issues involved in the Committee's terms of reference are of a most fundamental and far-reaching character. They involve not only the most complicated problems of technique and organization, but profound problems of a more theoretical or philosophical nature."

And yet, at the March 1953 meeting of the Federal Open Market Committee there was unanimous approval of the two most important statements of policy with respect to the operations of the System Open Market Account which had been suggested by the Ad Hoc Subcommittee. (Underlining supplied.)

> *(1)* <u>*Under present conditions,*</u> *operations for the System account should be confined to the short end of the market (not including correction of disorderly markets);*

> *(2) It is not now the policy of the Committee to support any pattern of prices and yields in the Government securities market, and intervention in the Government securities market is solely to effectuate the objectives of monetary and credit policy (including correction of disorderly markets).*

The second of these ordinances, which really should have been first, put a seal of disapproval on any future pegging of prices of Government securities such as had been practiced during World War II, and in the postwar period of readjustment in the Government securities market while the consequences of financing the war were being unwound. The first ordinance represented a consensus that, *in most circumstances*, the Open Market Committee would be able to attain its policy objectives by operating in the market for Treasury bills and other short-term Government securities.

The apple of discord became apparent later when there was a creeping movement to give constitutional permanence to the doctrine which had become known as "bills only", and to engrave it permanently in the public mind, and particularly in the minds of Government securities dealers, by a dribble of statements of individuals concerning the "ground rules" for all future open market operations, even though the question of publicizing ground rules had been deferred by the Open Market Committee for further study.

At the September 1953 meeting of the Open Market Committee[4] the phrase "under present conditions" was dropped from the directive that operations for System Account be confined to the short end of the market, and replaced by the clause "until such time as (it) may be superseded or modified by further action of the Federal Open Market Committee". And, at the December meeting of the Committee in 1953, the

[4] There was a June meeting of the Open Market Committee at which there were five presidents of Federal Reserve Banks and four members of the Board of Governors, and at which the March directive relating to confining operations for System Account to the short-term sector of the market was rescinded, with the understanding that the Executive Committee of the Federal Open Market Committee (which was later abolished) would be free to determine how operations should be carried on in the light of the current general credit policy of the full Open Market Committee. The five presidents voted for the motion to rescind and the four Board members voted against it (following the meeting, the Executive Committee, consisting of three Board members and two presidents, decided to confine *current* operations to Treasury bills). By the time of the September meeting of the Open Market Committee, three of the presidents had changed their minds concerning preserving such limited freedom of action and the March pronouncement, as amended, was restored by a vote of nine to two.

general statement with respect to System intervention in the Government securities market was changed to read "transactions for System account in the open market shall be entered into *solely for the purpose of providing or absorbing reserves, except in the correction of disorderly markets*".[5]

The major differences of opinion, at least within the Federal Open Market Committee, had now become (1) whether it was misleading and undesirable to promulgate a capsule version of the whole theory of central banking, and the whole purpose of open market operations, which mentioned only the providing and absorbing of reserves and omitted the essential linkage between such actions and the cost and availability of credit; (2) whether it was unnecessary and undesirable to endow the doctrine of "bills only" with an air of permanence as a norm of System open market operations, no matter what changes in economic conditions and in the market structure of interest rates might occur; (3) whether it was desirable to attempt to provide the Government securities dealers with a continuing set of "ground rules" for System open market operations, which would seek to protect the market from the hazards of there being a central banking system whose policy decisions, and whose every action to make its policy decisions effective, must influence the cost and availability of credit throughout the economy and, therefore, the movements of interest rates and prices through the whole range of maturities in the Government securities market.

In the running debate which followed, a great deal of discussion was devoted to elucidating the obvious necessity of having a properly functioning Government securities market in which to conduct System open market operations; to trying to prove that confining such operations to the short end of the maturity scale would improve, or had improved, the "breadth, depth, and resiliency" of the market; and to asserting that substitutability was more important than arbitrage in carrying impulses throughout the whole range of maturities. But the major questions involving the promulga-

---

[5] This change had a special application to so-called "swap" transactions in connection with Treasury financing, but it also was an attempt to nail down permanently a general philosophy of open market operations.

tion of a norm of central banking and the publication of permanent "ground rules" for the conduct of open market operations tended to be neglected, while the Federal Open Market Committee annually voted to perpetuate the views of its satisfied majority. It is ironical, perhaps, that the so-called "bills only" policy, which was hailed by one of its chief architects in October 1960 as "the greatest advance in central banking technique in the last decade", was overtaken by events and abandoned in February 1961. The Federal Open Market Committee then announced that the System Open Market Account was purchasing Government notes and bonds of varying maturities "in the light of conditions that have developed in the domestic economy and in the U.S. balance of payments". The question of "bills only" may arise again, of course; its abandonment can be endowed with no more real permanence than its adoption, but it is unlikely that it will ever be revived as the basis for the sweeping assertion that transactions for System Account in the open market shall be entered into solely for the purpose of providing or absorbing reserves.

It is reassuring on this score that the latest Joint Treasury-Federal Reserve Study of the U.S. Government Securities Market (April 1969) recommends that "System purchases of intermediate- and long-term U.S. Government coupon issues should be continued—even apart from use in correction or forestalling disorderly market conditions—as a useful supplement to bill purchases in providing reserves to the banking system and, when compelling reasons exist, for affecting to the extent consistent with reserve objectives interest rate pressures in specific short- or long-term maturity sectors of the debt market".

The mechanical purpose formula for Federal Reserve open market operations which grew out of the doctrine of "bills only" is a not too distant relative of what is, at the moment, the most virulent form of norm addiction, the "money supply" addiction. Both would rely wholly on market forces to produce desired effects flowing from Federal Reserve action affecting a single monetary aggregate. The present virulence of the money supply proposal for getting rid of the fallible judgment of central bankers, and substituting a mechanical formula for their gropings, may be ascribed to the existence of a "school" for the propagation of the faith and to a combination of circumstances relating to the respective merits of fiscal and monetary policy in helping order our economic affairs which has stirred up academic dispute and endowed the views of the "school" with a modicum of public attention and political acceptance.

Once an energetic and forensically formidable economist assembles a massive collection of empirical historical evidence to provide apparent support for his opinions, and indoctrinates enough disciples who then go forth and preach the gospel, a "school" becomes established. If there happens to be another "school" of followers of another leader whose views have found wide professional and political acceptance in the past, and which now may be attacked with some hope of success, the stage is set for a rash of academic and journalistic coverage of the battle. The whole subject then comes to the attention of a growing group of men of affairs in politics and in business, and the risk arises that a shaky hypothesis may become something more than a source of academic argument and journalistic enterprise.

We are not concerned here, however, as to whether Keynes or Friedman is the economic messiah of our time, but with the claim of the monetarists that the money supply should be the sole or, at least, the supreme norm of reference of monetary policy. We are concerned with the proposal that the Federal Reserve should content itself with attempting to increase the money supply at a fixed annual rate (4 or 5 percent a year is suggested) calculated on the average to be consistent with stable prices, thus providing a stable monetary framework in which other economic goals may be realized and avoiding the hazards of trying to use monetary policy as a flexible and sensitive instrument for influencing our economic affairs.

In the more restrained versions of this theory, it is admitted that monetary growth is not a precise and infallible source of future economic stability but that, on the average (which conceals much variability in both the time delay and the magnitude of the response), there is a close relationship between the rate of change in the quantity of money and the rate of change in national income (at current prices) some six months or more later.

This is an appealing doctrine which "rolls up into one simple explanatory variable all of the many complex forces which determine aggregate demand". No wonder political interest has been aroused and a public following has emerged. But the economic peers of the monetarists are skeptical. They have raised many questions concerning the money supply theory which the monetarists have yet to answer convincingly. Drawing on the work of those who have addressed themselves to the problem and are competent to discuss it as professional economists, I shall list some of these questions.

First and foremost is the question of whether the asserted causal connection between cycles of growth of the money stock and cyclical movements of the economy runs from money to business activity or from business activity to money. It is akin to the question phrased by a British writer: "Did man begin to lose his general covering of hair when he began wearing clothes, or did he begin wearing clothes when he noticed he was going into a permanent moult?"

Second, what monetary aggregate is to be used as the guide of monetary policy; is it the money stock narrowly defined as currency in circulation and demand deposits at banks, or is it currency and demand deposits plus time deposits at banks, or is it the "monetary base", or is it the money supply which is "currently most meaningful in indicating monetary influence in economic activity"? Recent revisions of the most commonly used money supply series, and the patent sketchiness of such series stretching back into the historical and statistical past ("over a century") add point to this basic question.

Third, are the econometric models which the monetarists use to demonstrate how the transmission process proceeds from money to business activity adequate for the purpose?

Fourth, are not both price and quantity of money important; do you not have to take into account shifts in demand and in interest rates?

Fifth, do the observed variations in monetary time lags and monetary velocity cast doubts on the suggested simple causal relationship between the money supply and general economic activity; do they not suggest that there are unpredictable variables other than the money supply which influence the level of economic activity and which must be taken into account in devising monetary policy?

Sixth, the suggested monetary framework for the economy is put forward most precisely in terms of a closed economy, although it is admitted that it should involve a free foreign exchange market (floating exchange rates) in the open economy of which this country actually is a part. Is this a practical directive for monetary policy?

Even if some of these murky areas are cleared and the monetarists become less rigid in their formulations, experience suggests that the money supply norm of central bank policy eventually will take its place on the library shelves along with the policy norms of the past. With improvement of our knowledge and understanding of the present state of the economy and its likely future course, the money supply norm may leave a trace; the use of annual rates of change in the money supply as a navigational aid for central bank action (channel markers indicating maximum and minimum rates of growth to be sought) cannot be ruled out, but the discretionary band would have to be wide enough to accommodate the flexible requirements dictated by experience.

Practicing central bankers (and the governments to which they are responsible) cannot afford to be confined by formulae which attempt to cope, in precise measure, with the actions and anticipations of millions of human beings exercising a high degree of economic freedom of choice. Monetary policy can continue to make its contribution to the goals of vigorous sustainable economic growth, maximum attainable production and employment, and reasonable stability of prices, if its practitioners continue to sharpen their analyses of complex economic developments and continue to base their actions upon a balanced view of total situations. They cannot be relieved of this difficult task by doctrinaire policy norms.

Testimony on "Bills Only" before the Subcommittee on Economic Stabilization of the Joint Committee on the Economic Report, December 7, 1954

I am going to speak of something which I am sure is not the major concern of your hearing, just as it is not the major concern of the Federal Open Market Committee, but nevertheless it is something which I do not think was covered, from my point of view, in the answers submitted to you by the Chairman of the Board of Governors and, therefore, if I may take your time, I would like to refer to it. It is, perhaps, what might be called the negative, in answer to your question number three.*

Your subcommittee addressed five questions to the Chairman of the Board of Governors, and his answers have been made available to other participants in these hearings, as well as to the public.

With respect to the answers to questions 1, 2, 4, and 5, I am in general and substantial agreement, even though there might be some shades of difference of opinion or degrees of emphasis in answers to the same questions which I might prepare.

This suggests the first point I would like to make: So far as general credit policy is concerned, there has been a high degree of unanimity within the Federal Reserve System throughout the period covered by your inquiry, that is, since March 1951.

Our differences, or my differences with other members of the Federal Open Market Committee, have related to the techniques of open market operations, not to general credit policies.

* *Editor's note:* Question 3 was: "What is the practical significance of shifting policy emphasis from the view of 'maintaining orderly conditions' to the view of 'correcting disorderly situations' in the securities market? What were the considerations leading the Open Market Committee to confine its operations to the short end of the market (not including correction of disorderly markets)? What has been the experience with operations under this decision?"

It is to these questions of techniques that your question No. 3 is directed. Here again I can express a good deal of agreement with much that is included in the answer of the chairman. It is a persuasive and stimulating discussion of the issues involved. Yet there is also a good deal with which I disagree, and my conclusions as to the most effective use of open market operations, to implement credit policy and to promote economic growth and stability, diverge quite sharply from those set forth in the answer of the Chairman.

His answer is, of course, responsive to the question of the subcommittee, which asked for affirmative support of the actions of the Federal Open Market Committee to which it refers, not for the arguments for and against such actions.

Obviously, there is not time here for a full-dress presentation of the negative side of the question. I should like to make certain points which, I think, are significant to an understanding of the problem, however, and I should be glad to submit to the committee later, if it so desires, a written statement of views which might match the answer of the chairman in completeness and, I would hope, in persuasiveness.

First, as a matter of background, I think I should say that I am not for pegging Government securities prices nor for trying continuously to determine the structure of interest rates by means of open market operations. As one of the principals in the fight to free the Federal Reserve System from the pegging of prices of Government securities, throughout a difficult period of controversy on this point, beginning in 1946, I think I have the right to make this clear. And, as one who has a great deal of respect for the operations of the marketplace, I would not want to be classed with those who believe that a continuously better result can be obtained, so far as the structure of interest rates is concerned, by completely substituting the judgment of the Federal Open Market Committee for the marketplace. If we want to find out how the patient is doing, there must be some place where we can take the patient's pulse.

Now, taking up the real issues in this minor problem. The least controversial issue was dropping from the directive of the Federal Open Market Committee the clause authorizing open market operations to maintain orderly conditions in the market for Government securities, and substituting for it a clause authorizing operations to correct disorderly situations in the market. I voted in favor of this change, and thought it desirable, not just as a question of semantics. But I would stress the avoidance of disorderly situations rather than their correction after they have happened.

One of the virtues of credit control is supposed to be its ability to take prompt action to head off financial disturbances which might otherwise have harmful repercussions throughout the economy. If open market operations in longer term Government securities can be used to this end, I would use them rather than wait until a disorderly situation or a crisis has developed, and only then depart from operations solely in Treasury bills.

The most controversial issue was the instruction by the Federal Open Market Committee that open market operations must be confined to the short end of the Government securities market, except in correcting disorderly situations which, in practice, has come to mean confining operations to Treasury bills. I did not get the impression that the action was merely an assertion of the power of the Federal Open Market Committee to determine whether and when the System Open Market Account should engage in transactions outside the short end of the market. There need not be any question of the power of the full committee to determine the conditions and the general timing of operations in the longer term areas of the market.

I was concerned with the strong emphasis which I thought was given to permanence of the "bills only" doctrine. Suggestions for publishing a set of rules of the game, references to a constitution for open market operations, and the repeated argument that Government securities dealers could not create a broad, continuous market if we did not forego operations in long-term securities—except to correct disorderly conditions—gave me the disturbing impression that we were in danger of placing ourselves in a straitjacket which would not permit us to accomplish what the Congress and the public might expect us to accomplish in terms of monetary management.

I, therefore, welcomed the statement in the answer of the chairman to your question No. 3 that the door is being kept open to a change in the present basic technique of open market operations, and the recognition in his answer that the present approach to open market operations is still experimental and that insufficient time has elapsed to draw firm conclusions as to its performance. The publication of these views should help dispel the idea that present techniques have been adopted for all time, and should help to avoid further hardening of the dangerous opinion that any future operations by the System in the long-term market will be the signal of a critical situation.

I also welcome the repeated references, in the answer of the chairman, to the concern of credit policy with developments in the long-term sector of the market and the assertion of the particular concern of the Federal Open Market Committee that its policies be reflected in the cost and availability of credit in the long-term markets. It has been, and still is, my contention that this concern can find its best expression, at times, in open market operations specifically directed at these longer term markets.

This is, perhaps, the variant approach to open market operations briefly commented upon, and summarily dismissed, beginning on page 20 of the answers of the chairman to your question No. 3. As set forth there, it is described as a method of operation in which—

> the Federal Open Market Committee would normally permit the interplay of market forces to register on prices and rates in all of the various securities sectors of the market, but would stand ready to intervene with direct purchases, sales, or swaps in any sector where market developments took a trend that the committee considered was adverse to high-level economic stability.

That seems to me to be an eminently reasonable approach to our problem, but it has never really been tried—not even in the period 1951-53 to which the chairman refers. And now it has been dismissed on what I believe is the shaky assumption that it "did not appear to offer real promise of removing obstacles to improvement in the technical behavior of the market".

This probably brings us down to the nub of the differences. The Chairman's answer to your question No. 3 embraces the view, with which I agree, that the "depth, breadth, and resiliency" of the Government securities market, or its "continuity and responsiveness", should be furthered by all means that are consistent with a credit policy of maximum effectiveness, and that, in general, the greater the "depth, breadth, and resiliency" of the market, the greater will be the scope and opportunity for effective credit control through open market operations. But the proof of that pudding must be found in the actual market, not in a theoretical discussion of a supposedly ideal market.

The answer of the Chairman asserts that the market has become increasingly stronger, broader, and more resilient since the Committee adopted the "bills only" technique. It suggests most persuasively why, theoretically, this should be so. But it does not prove that it has actually happened. In fact, I wonder whether we are talking about the same market, and what are the definitions of "strength" and "breadth" that are being used. It is my information and observation that the market for longer term securities has remained at least as "thin", under existing open market procedures, as it was before these procedures were adopted.

I think it has lost depth, breadth, and resiliency, whether you view it in terms of dealer willingness to take position risks, volume of trading, or erratic price movements. We must not be misled by the claims of one or two dealers who urge the present techniques and now proclaim that they are helping to create a broader market for Government securities.

I do not think we have helped to create such a market. And, therefore, I do not see how the responsiveness of cost and availability of credit in all sectors of the market since June 1953 can have been the result of a progressive strengthening of the Government securities market growing out of the actions of the Open Market Committee with respect to the open market techniques. Much of the success of the System's actions during this period has derived from the promptness of adaptation of overall credit policy to changes in the economic situation, and to a high degree of coordination of Federal fiscal policy and debt management with credit policy. For the rest, it has sometimes taken massive releases of reserves, under the techniques adopted or in support of those techniques, to accomplish what might have been accomplished more economically with the help of limited direct entry into the long-term market.

I am hopeful, therefore, that the present period of experimentation will not be too long extended, and that we shall soon have an opportunity to experiment with the middle way—the variant approach—which I mentioned earlier.

One final comment should be made, perhaps, in connection with your question 3 on the discontinuance by the Federal Open Market Committee of direct supporting operations in the Government's securities market during periods of Treasury financing.

I would agree that the System Open Market Account should not, as a matter of routine, provide such direct support, but I would also say that we cannot, as a matter of routine, turn our back on such support.

The emphasis in the present approach to Treasury financing is good. The Treasury should meet the test of the market, in relation to other credit needs of the economy, to the fullest possible extent. But too rigid application of this doctrine is questionable as a matter of market procedure and Treasury-Federal Reserve relationships. In periods of credit ease, when policy considerations point to the need of keeping Treasury demands from draining credit away from desirable private use, reliance on bill purchases alone may lead to unwanted consequences. The flooding of funds into the bill market, in order to assure adequate credit in the areas tapped by the Treasury, may produce an undue enlargement of bank reserves, or an extreme distortion in Treasury bill prices and yields, or both.

There will also be times, particularly in periods of credit restraint, as distinguished from the recent period of overall credit ease, when rigid application of the present rule may result in serious collisions of debt management and credit policy, which might have been avoided without jeopardizing the overall public interest.

Now, let me repeat, what I have been discussing are disagreements over techniques of open market operations, not over general credit policy. It is good to have these differences opened up, and I hope that this hearing will result in more discussions of the problems involved by an informed public. We in the Federal Reserve System cannot consider ourselves to be the sole repositories of knowledge in these matters. What I have been most afraid of is that we might come to think that we can indulge in the luxury of a fixed idea. There is no such easy escape from specific and empirical decisions in central banking. We cannot have a general formula, a kind of economic law, which will serve the ends of credit policy under all sorts of economic conditions.

Letter to Murray J. Rossant

February 28, 1961

Dear Mr. Rossant:

Your letter of February 24 was a welcome reminder that there are some people who remember the "bills preferably" controversy of a few years ago and my part in it. I am delighted that time and circumstance have now combined to persuade the Federal Open Market Committee to do what I failed to persuade it to do by repeated votes of eleven to one. The chairman has been fond of saying that the task of a central bank is to lean against the wind. The Federal Reserve System is now leaning with the wind.

I think that the proponents of "bills preferably" painted themselves into a corner with the idea that there must be a "norm" to guide a central bank in its decisions and that "bills preferably" provided the key to such a norm. Having adapted this bit of economic lore to their needs, they were hell-bent to publish "the rules of the game" so that change would not be easy. This was vetoed by the Federal Open Market Committee, but it was soon leaked out that there were "rules of the game" which destroyed the residue of flexibility which was piously proclaimed. The arguments that the alternative to "bills preferably" was pegging, and that to deal in longer term securities meant trying to establish the whole structure of interest rates, were trotted out to silence the opposition by trying to make its position one of subservience to the needs of the Treasury or an absurdity. I think that the independence of the Federal Reserve System has been damaged, but not irreparably, by its intransigence in this whole business. It is now believed to be following the election returns as well as changing economic conditions.

The moaning of the Government securities dealers I would attribute largely to the sounds emanating from Lanston and Co., which had quite a bit to do with the adoption of "bills preferably". The rest of them talked out of both sides of their mouths, and went ahead making money in the Government market, as is their business. The banks, of course, kept mum for fear of offending somebody.

I shouldn't think anyone would expect miracles of this change in the operating techniques of the System, but I do hope that the revived freedom to operate in all sections of the market will be used effectively in situations in which it can be useful, such as the present. Combined with appropriate debt management, quite a bit can be accomplished.

I am still working on the 1952, 1953, and 1955 wines, but I have no doubt that some of the 1959 whites are now ready for drinking and good, and I shall be into them shortly.

With best regards.

Sincerely,

Allan Sproul

Letter to Alfred Hayes

March 14, 1961

Dear Al:

Thank you for your letter of March 3, and now for your letter of March 10. I am glad to know that one of the brethren supported you "most of the way" in the Federal Open Market Committee, but the vote was always eleven to one, as I recall.

The problem of imaginary history, one-sided explanations, either/or presentations, and dubious allies, in the battle of "bills only" has bothered me over the years, as it has you. I still think that you were right, as an individual and in setting policy for the Bank, not to engage in a public debate on the matter, after my abortive attempt to stir up public interest in what was being done. I think I was right not to take up the argument, again, after leaving the System. I had two reasons. One, I did not wish to be an embarrassment to the New York Bank, which had to make up its mind and then press its views within the Committee, under your direction. Two, I have observed that, usually, he who continues the attack after he has left the fighting forces is likely to lose his audiences pretty quickly. That has not meant that I did not feel free to make my views known, and thus to keep them alive, whenever they were sought by individuals, publications, committees, and commissions.

As one result of the partial blackout of conflicting views during the past few years, the present reversal of policy, as you point out, has been the subject of new distortions by the uninformed (e.g., Arthur Krock) and violent attacks by the informed partisans of "bills only", and it has encouraged embarrassing allies. There were some monetary analysts who opposed "bills only" in the past, however, and I would expect them and others to be more vocal in opposing a return to that doctrine if it is attempted. I would also expect that you and others would have a chance to oppose it within the System, and before Congressional committees, with a much better chance of success than in the past. I shall certainly now feel free to say and write what I think about the past and about the future for whatever that may be worth. I have a lot of material which I have been collecting during the period of silence!

Quite apart from the technical merits or demerits of "bills only", I think it was a great mistake for the Federal Open Market Committee to let itself become enamoured of so-called "rules of the game", which were to be the ten commandments of central banking—carved in stone. These rules made a pious fraud of protestations of flexibility and contributed to intellectual dishonesty in pretending to study and discuss the question of "bills only". I am disturbed, therefore, that some defenders of the Federal Reserve are saying that the abandonment of "bills only" is a temporary expedient and an experiment, and that the System will return to "bills only" as soon as we are rid of a domestic recession and a balance-of-payments deficit. I would hate to see the System get back into the straitjacket.

With best regards.

Sincerely,

Allan

Letter to Henry Alexander

Zurich
April 17, 1961

Mr. Henry Alexander
Chairman of the Board
Morgan Guaranty Trust Company

Dear Henry:

It is a partial holiday in Zurich and so this letter. I have read the exercise in statistical calisthenics which was included in the April Survey of your bank, which you gave me when I had the pleasure of dining with you last Thursday noon. It seems to me that it shows considerable ingenuity in demonstrating that if you resolve all, or nearly all, of the influences which affect interest rates at short and long term in the actual money and capital markets, both as to timing and amplitude of savings, there is convincing evidence of a high degree of "covariation". Even then, there was a lack of "covariation" in 1955 and early 1956, which had to be explained—an exception to prove the rule, I suppose.

As an attack on the decision of the Federal Reserve System to abandon the doctrine of "bills preferably", which this article will be considered by many, it is less than convincing no matter what its excellence for other purposes may be. It sets up a misleading basis of debate, namely the degree of linkage between short and long term interest rates over the whole of the business cycle, and then proceeds to show "the realities of the case" by its own variety of statistical analysis.

The first general rule of central banking is that statistical analysis can never carry you to the heart of an economic problem requiring prompt decisions before all the statistics of the past have been gathered and analyzed over days, weeks, and months. You need all the information you can get, analyzed as competently as possible, and then you need to make some human judgments which are still beyond the range of electric computers.

To be more specific, the discussion of monetary policy, as it relates to "bills preferably" has not centered in the degree of linkage between short and long rates over the whole of the business cycle, and it has not been assumed that long-term rates have been *continuously* sluggish in their response to changes in the business cycle and to the force of monetary policy. It has been claimed that, at times, the linkage may be less rapid than would be desirable in terms of effective monetary policy, and that the Federal Reserve System should be free, at such times, to intervene directly in the intermediate- or long-term market for Government securities, to try to ascertain if there is some temporary friction or if it is misjudging the force of fundamental factors—in which case it can withdraw.

If the monetary authorities are properly concerned with the whole interest rate structure, as it may affect the flow of credit and capital into productive use, as I think they must be, it accomplishes little to prove a high degree of "covariation" over periods as long as the ordinary business cycle, or to extract "obscuring influences" which are themselves obscured by actions of the monetary authorities. For example, on page 3, where the article says seasonal patterns of interest rates have been gradually reemerging and "reflect for the most part the extent to which the central banking system does not elect to cancel out the rhythmic changes within the year in the credit demands of business and government". The dog is chasing its tail!

As I see it, the monetary authorities responded to a compelling set of circumstances in announcing on February 20 that they had abandoned the doctrine of "bills preferably". And the circumstances were properly more compelling than the "volatility pattern characteristic of each (short and long rates) over a prolonged period of observation". Those who have spoken for the System have made it clear that they have no preconceived or fixed rate relationships in mind, and that they do not intend to try to force the market in a direction counter to that determined by the underlying demand and supply conditions, and they have shown that they have a problem of the rate structure growing partly out of the concentration of their open market operations in the bill market.

In the relatively new world of widespread currency convertibility, which encourages the flow of short-term funds between international money markets in response to interest rate differentials, and in the light of a balance-of-payments position which showed substantial deficits and triggered a flight from the dollar, and in the face of a domestic economic situation which called for an easy money policy, the monetary authorities needed to free themselves from their self-imposed rule of dealing only, or largely, in Treasury bills. At the same time, they were justified in seeking to find out if operations in other sectors of the market might beneficially hasten "covariation" even though the frictions in the market "are minimal under normal circumstance" whenever that is.

It is significant that, even with free reserves in the banking system maintained at a level of about $500 million, short-term rates have remained at figures which, together with some reduction of rates in foreign money centers, have removed most or all of the incentives to send short-term funds abroad for interest rate reasons. Equally significant, perhaps, is the fact that open market operations in the intermediate area have facilitated some extension of the Federal debt, which becomes shorter all the time if you don't do something about it. And, finally, despite a number of influences which might readily have pushed up long-term rates, such rates have remained fairly steady during the past two months, suggesting that they have remained as low as was consistent with underlying market factors, without interfering with the flow of savings into productive use as witnessed by the heavy calendar of securities flotations. This is what the discussion of "bills preferably" has been about; not about buying "to force the movements (of rates) apart for any prolonged period".

Quite apart from the merits or demerits of "bills preferably" under "normal" circumstances, I think the Federal Reserve System should not again paint itself into a corner so that responses to "abnormal" circumstances require elaborate explanation and make changes in a technique of operation seem to be an important change of policy.

The elevation of "bills preferably" to a great new principle of central banking which must be engraved on tablets of stone, for all time, was a presumptuous thing. The undoing of this presumption is no matter of experiment or expedience, but a return to the real world. The episode should be buried.

I hope you can and will read this (Miss Regan at the Reserve Bank will decipher and type it for you if necessary, I am sure).

With all the best,

Sincerely,

Allan

P.S. How about getting the statisticians to study the "covariation" of the prime rate and other short-term rates? From the 1959-60 high to early April 1961, it had declined from 5 to 4½ percent while three-month Treasury bills were going down from 4.67 to 2.47 and one-year issues from 5.15 to 2.97. Stickiness seems to be more than minimal here!

The Second Annual Arthur K. Salomon Lecture delivered at the Graduate School of Business of New York University on November 7, 1963

Money Will Not Manage Itself

It is a sobering circumstance for me to find myself speaking from this platform from which my friend, the late Per Jacobsson, delivered the first Arthur K. Salomon Lecture a year ago. That vigorous and wide-ranging Swedish internationalist talked of monetary matters in terms of time and place, of theory and practice, with a command which only he could bring to the discussion of world monetary problems. I think it appropriate on this occasion to register my respect for his accomplishments and my affection for the man.

The thoughts on monetary management which I shall place before you will be narrower than his in compass and less extensive in time. They will relate primarily to central banking in the United States now and during the past fifty years, although the title I have given my talk comes from a "foreign" book, the writing of which was begun nearly a hundred years ago. You will have recognized it as the catchline from the most famous book on central banking, Walter Bagehot's "Lombard Street". Just as any economist worth his salt will mention the name of Adam Smith sometime in his discourse or in his writings, so a central banker gains character by associating his views and reflections with those of a man who wrote about the London money market and the Bank of England in 1870-73, especially if he agrees with the dictum that "money will not manage itself" as he almost must by reason of his calling.

I have two other reasons for launching my remarks with Bagehot's words. On another occasion, when I delivered myself of opinions which questioned the sanctity of the "old" Gold Standard, a disputatious merchant of this city published a pamphlet with the intriguing title "Sproul Ignores Common Honesty". In it he included this priceless definition of monetary management: "A high-sounding euphemism; it means constant lying to support constant swindling." I rather liked that or I would not have remembered it.

And, finally, there is the fact that it is just fifty years since the Congress of the United States passed the Federal Reserve Act, which created the Federal Reserve System. A semicentennial bow to monetary management in the United States suggests itself as appropriate to this gathering.

Perhaps it will advance the clarity of my discussion if I quickly sketch in a little banking history. And here I shall rely largely on what others have written, because I am going back one hundred years and my own association with these matters does not go back that far. The National Currency Act, signed by President Lincoln in 1863, which authorized the incorporation of national banks; and the National Bank Act of 1864, which amended and improved the Currency Act; and the Federal Reserve Act of 1913 are the high marks of progress in our banking legislation over the past century. The national banking legislation of one hundred years ago knitted together the badly raveled banking system of the country and provided us with the beginnings of a controlled circulating medium which the United States had lacked since the Jacksonians destroyed the Second Bank of the United States in the 1830s. Men's minds in the 1860s were concentrated on bank notes, however, and the national banking legislation did not take much account of the role of bank deposits, and the bank check, in the money supply of the nation. It left the Federal Government with powers less than its responsibilities and its needs. The Federal Reserve Act of 1913 moved to complete what had been started fifty years before, namely the provision of a uniform and generally acceptable currency and national regulation of the money supply. The issuance of our principal form of currency, the Federal Reserve note, and the means of regulating the money supply, by way of the volume of demand (and time) deposits in the commercial banks of the country, were placed in the hands of the Federal Reserve System.

That was a determination that there was to be a degree of monetary management in the United States. But, because of ancient prejudices and still lively suspicions, and because of an awareness of the fallibility of human foresight and human judgment, it was thought that this power could be substantially divorced from acts of discretion. The reserve creating and destroying powers of the Federal Reserve System, which are the means by which it controls bank deposits, were to respond to changes in the country's gold supply and to the discount by member banks of self-liquidating paper. Changes in the production of gold, the international balance of payments, and the rise and fall of the self-generated credit needs of agriculture, commerce, and industry were to determine, pretty largely, the amounts of Reserve Bank credit which would come into being or go out of existence.

This groping for an automatic means of monetary influence on economic affairs sometimes changes its form, but never its substance. And so long as human beings disagree as to what has been done, and what might have been done, and what should have been done, in a variety of particular circumstances, it probably never will be abandoned. It is now generally accepted, I believe, that monetary policy has power to stimulate, stabilize, and restrain the economy and should be used to these ends. But, since the reasons for action are seldom clear and conclusive, and the conflicting currents in the economy must be analyzed and interpreted by men who lack perfect foresight, the quest for an automatic guide to affirmative action goes on.

The simplest form of this yearning is the nostalgic belief of many people that a return to the Gold Standard, as they believe it existed during the years 1880 to 1914, would be the means of our salvation. They seem to think, and I have to confess to having shared the opinion in my salad days, that monetary policy as it existed in the brief thirty-four years of the "golden era" was essentially automatic (except, perhaps, to some extent in the case of the Bank of England), involving mostly mechanical responses to international gold movements and a minimum of discretionary action directed toward influencing such movements or toward influencing domestic economic conditions. As Professor Arthur Bloomfield, of the University of Pennsylvania, has developed in his notable studies of this period, this is a misconception. Although we know much less than we used to think we did about the actual functioning of the pre-1914 Gold Standard, Professor Bloomfield's studies of central bank action in that period suggest strongly that the monetary authorities "did not consistently follow any simple or single rule or criterion of policy, or focus exclusively on considerations of convertibility, but they were constantly called upon to exercise, and did exercise, their judgment on such matters as whether or not to act in any given situation and, if so, at what point of time to act, the kind and extent of action to take, and the instrument or instruments of policy to use". And they had to contend with many of the problems with which central bankers have to contend today including, in the international sphere, disruptive movements of short-term funds from country to country, destabilizing exchange speculation, capital flights threatening the maintenance of convertibility, and concern as to the adequacy of international reserves. All they lacked to be modern, it seems, were the directions which central banks have now received from their governments, explicitly or implicitly, concerning national economic objectives (such as the Employment Act of 1946 in our case), and some of the statistical information and analytical tools which central bankers now have to help them discharge their responsibilities, and some means of executing policy, domestic and international, which central bankers have devised by way of open market operations in Government securities and cooperative arrangements for stabilizing the foreign exchanges. A return to the mixture of the variants of the Gold Standard which existed in much of the Western world from 1880 to 1914 could not free us from the mistakes of men. And this would hold, whether we maintained the present price of gold, or doubled it, or tripled it in order to increase international liquidity with one hand, while we destroyed it with the other by destroying confidence in the dollar and sterling (or any currency) as an international reserve currency.

The search for a more effective and practical guide than the old Gold Standard to monetary automation under present-day conditions is most ardently pursued, I suppose, by Professor Milton Friedman of the University of Chicago who has said that "what we need is not a skilled driver of the economic vehicle continuously turning the steering wheel to adjust to unexpected irregularities of the route, but some means of keeping the monetary passenger, who is in the back seat as ballast, from occasionally leaning over and giving the steering wheel a jerk that threatens to send the car off the road". The steering device which he suggests, in lieu of this back seat driver, is a steady 3 or 4 percent week-by-week and month-by-month increase in the stock of money (not easily to be defined accurately) to accommodate an expanding need which arises from a growing population, increases in per capita output and income, and increases in the proportion of income directed to liquidity, all of which call for an increase in the money supply to prevent a continually falling price level.

Professor Friedman has assembled massive statistical support, chosen by him, to show that the monetary authorities in the United States have most often been wrong in their acts of discretion, and that when they seemed to be right it was usually by mistake. I find it impossible to swallow his prescription which would reduce monetary management to the definitive act of forcing a constant drip of money into the economic blood stream. It seems to me to be patent that the uncertain hand of man is needed in a world of uncertainties and change and human beings, to try to accommodate the performance of the monetary system to the needs of particular times and circumstances and people. I here agree with Professor Samuelson, of the Massachusetts Institute of Technology, who has written that a "definitive mechanism, which is to run forever after, by itself, involves a single act of discretion which transcends, in both its arrogance and its capacity for potential harm, any repeated acts of foolish discretion that can be imagined".

It is not my purpose to argue that the Federal Reserve System has not made mistakes in the past fifty years, nor that it may not make mistakes in the future. The early attempts of the System to preserve a distinction between essential and nonessential, or between speculative and constructive, uses of Federal Reserve credit now appear naive. The attempt to preserve a distinction between the elasticity of the components of the money supply, currency and demand deposits, was misguided. The exercises in moral suasion and direct pressure were largely futile. The resort to "bills only" or "bills preferably" as a technique of open market operations, thus trying to forswear action to influence directly any part of the interest rate structure except at the short end, was an eight-year aberration. There has been timidity approaching irresolution with respect to selective credit controls, and many recurring actions designed to stimulate or restrain or stabilize the economy can be and have been criticized. What I am saying is that over the past fifty years there have been improvements, and I am confident there will be more. Some primitive beliefs concerning money have been discarded, the collection and analysis of economic statistics have steadily improved, the organizational arrangements and the decision-making powers of our central banking system, despite some bad stretches, have evolved in the right direction.

I make the latter statement with full realization, I think, of the hazards which beset such arrangements and processes, especially when the political capital of the country and the private financial capital of the country are 220 miles apart on the map, and sometimes much further apart in their thinking about money matters. Per Jacobsson used to tell some of his central banking friends abroad that we have a funny central banking system in the United States; that most of the power is lodged in Washington and most of the knowledge in New York. He was indulging his wit at the expense of truth, of course, but it is wise to remember that the first and most direct point of contact between the policies of the monetary authorities and national and international money and capital markets is in New York.

As I have said before, this is no device of greedy men and no mere accident of geography which can be changed by legislative or administrative fiat, even if the fiat be called "driving the money changers from the temple". It reflects the necessity in a money economy, such as ours, of having a marketplace where the final and balancing transactions of our national and international financial accounts can be carried out by a variety of financial institutions, with connections which span the country and the world. And the operating arm of the Federal Reserve System in this money and capital market is the Federal Reserve Bank of New York.

Fortunately, it seems to me, we have been largely successful in overcoming this organizational hazard by one of those strokes of evolutionary genius which, more often than flashes of pure inspiration, bless our kind of society. Out of early attempts to find a way to use and coordinate the open market powers of the Federal Reserve Banks and to bring these powers within the ambit of the Board of Governors at Washington, the Federal Open Market Committee evolved. It has become the heart of the Federal Reserve System, although the shorthand of the press has created a public image of a Federal Reserve System wholly dominated by its Washington center. On the contrary, the Federal Open Market Committee recognizes a Federal association in a national authority, without sacrificing the ability to formulate and to execute necessary national policies. It is the forum where representatives of the constituent parts of the Federal Reserve System meet as individuals and equals, having identical responsibilities under law, to decide questions of high monetary policy with respect to open market operations in Government securities and foreign currencies, and to consider the coordination of these operations with discount rate policy and other policy measures. And, finally, the present constitution of the Federal Open Market Committee, with the President of the Federal Reserve Bank of New York as a statutory permanent member, observes a cardinal principle of central banking that those who determine monetary policy should not only coordinate their actions with the general economic policies of the government, but should also have direct contact with the private money market—a contact which comes from living in the market, and being able to feel the pulse of the market by dealing in it, and by keeping in personal touch with the individuals and institutions whose composite actions help to determine how monetary policy will be transmitted to the whole economy through the marketplace.

I reaffirm, then, my belief in the art and practice of money management, and I place my hopes for the future in improvement of the tools we have to use in practicing the art, and in the experience we gain in using them.

• • • • • • •

And now, in conclusion, let me return to my general theme: "money will not manage itself". It needs managers who are aware of the fact that they are dealing primarily with problems of human motivation and human reactions, and that some public understanding of what they are trying to do is a necessary ingredient of success. It needs managers who realize that "scientific analysis, unaided, can never carry the inquirer to the heart of an economic situation". It needs managers who "operate in the light of all the information they can get" and have it "organized and analyzed in such a way as to give the maximum amount of illumination", so that the available alternatives are clearly presented. And it needs managers who then remember that their tasks require "that practical wisdom which comes only from experience".

As I recall the past fifty years of development of the Federal Reserve System, I am reasonably sanguine about the future of money management in the United States. The system has proved to be a constructive public invention and a useful public servant. It has had a variety of experience. It should be ready for the work ahead.

An economist, who has achieved the rare distinction of having one of his books become a "best seller", gave a chapter in that book to the "monetary illusion", in which he expounded "the charm which this mysterious thing called monetary policy has for those who are privy to its practices, and whose affection for it is translated into claims for its effectiveness which invade the supernatural". "No other economic policy", he wrote, "has ever shown such capacity to survive failure, to be hailed as a success." This may be witty, but I reject the indictment. The practitioners of monetary policy are not exorbitant in their claims of effectiveness and usefulness. The primary function of monetary policy, with due allowance for the liquidity of the economy, is to regulate the total supply of money and to influence its cost and availability so as to help keep marginal demands—government and private—from spending themselves in speculation and increased prices in times of prosperity, and from being stifled in times of recession. In this way, it contributes importantly to stability of the price level and stability of the exchange rate of the dollar, and to the attainment of maximum employment and sustainable growth. Monetary management cannot reach all the causes of economic instability, nor can it insure sustained high levels of employment and high rates of growth. But, combined with fiscal policy and wage-price policy, it is our best hope of preserving our freedom from the straitjacket of more direct governmental control of economic affairs. We must not cross over into the barren lands of the enemy.

Chapter 5

Deposit Interest Rate Ceilings

This chapter contains three of Sproul's letters and an excerpt from one of his talks, all on the subject of deposit interest rate ceilings.

By way of background, when the Federal Reserve Act was passed in 1913, it contained no provision of any sort fixing maximum permissible interest rates that banks could pay on deposits. At that time, this was not considered an appropriate area of regulation. Twenty years later, however, in the Banking Act of 1933, the Congress instructed the Federal Reserve to set rate ceilings on commercial bank time and savings deposits (Regulation Q), and prohibited entirely the payment of interest on demand deposits (a rate ceiling of zero).

The ceilings were imposed on the grounds that alleged excessive interest rate competition for deposits during the 1920s had undermined the soundness of the banking system. It was believed that competition to attract depositors had driven deposit interest rates up so high that the banks, burdened by the higher costs, were led to acquire high-yielding but excessively risky low-quality assets. It was held that this contributed to the collapse of the banking system in the early 1930s. Similar arguments were responsible for the imposition of comparable ceilings on mutual savings banks and savings and loan associations starting in 1966.

Until the early 1960s, the ceilings on time and savings deposit interest rates were hardly noticed, since they were always raised by the Federal Reserve whenever they became meaningful—that is, when short-term market interest rates threatened to rise above the ceilings. Above-ceiling short-term interest rates would tempt depositors to shift funds out of savings deposits and into money market instruments, such as Treasury bills. In 1966, however, the ceilings were not raised: instead, similar ceilings were imposed by the Congress on mutual savings banks and savings and loan associations and the ceilings were *lowered* despite rising open market rates. Since then, deposit interest rate ceilings have been one of the more controversial elements on the American banking scene.

Sproul began to question the wisdom of deposit rate ceilings rather early. In May 1960, in a letter reprinted below, he wrote to Alfred Hayes, his successor as president of the New York Bank: "It seems to me that it is time to assume that the banks are grown up and able to determine how much they can safely pay on savings deposits without going wild in making loans and investments . . . .I am thinking that it is time the System recommended to the Congress that the power to fix this ceiling be rescinded, leaving the banks free to make their individual decisions. Many bankers may not like this, for one reason or another, but they shouldn't expect to snuggle under Government coverlets when it pleases them and to howl about Government interference with business when it doesn't."

By 1966 his position had become even stronger. In a speech before a joint session of the American Finance Association and the American Economic Association, reprinted below, he concluded: "These attempts to fix interest rates and to direct savings flows have helped cause some of the most rapid and disruptive shifts in rates and in savings flows that we have ever experienced. It is hard to see how market forces could have done a worse job. Now we have our hand in a pocketful of fish hooks and it is going to be impossible to get it out without pain and discomfort."

Letter to Alfred Hayes

May 8, 1960

Dear Al:

I am assuming that you are back from your European trip, full of vigor and new ideas.

I have some ideas about the statutory and regulatory control of interest rates paid by commercial banks that I would like to put up to you people before I stick out my own neck.

The rate ceiling on savings deposits. It seems to me that it is time to assume that the banks are grown up and able to determine how much they can safely pay on savings deposits without going wild in making loans and investments. Given the changes in the condition of the banking system and in the climate of banking, since this regulatory power was given to the Board, the quality of bank supervision, and the favored competition of other thrift institutions, the commercial banks should not be forced to climb into the ring with one hand in a sling. Continuance of the present sluggish manipulation of the regulated ceiling is not fair to them, and a more flexible use of the ceiling would be tantamount to having the Board fix the rate. I am thinking that it is time the System recommended to the Congress that the power to fix this ceiling be rescinded, leaving the banks free to make their individual decisions.

Many bankers may not like this, for one reason or another, but they shouldn't expect to snuggle under Government coverlets when it pleases them and to howl about Government interference with business when it doesn't.

Payment of interest on demand deposits. The passage of time, with its changes in conditions and climate, affects this statutory control also. Of particular significance are the rise in the Treasury bill to the position of the chief liquidity instrument of the economy, the large volume of foreign short-term funds in this market, and the awakening of the treasurers of large corporations and of state and municipal financial officers from their long slumber. As you well know, funds now flow in and out of deposits at banks and into and out of Treasury bills with almost the predictability of the tides.

The Government securities dealers, with their corporate repurchase deals, have stepped into the picture. Why shouldn't banks make repurchase deals with their depositors who are interested in Treasury bills, or why shouldn't they buy and sell Treasury bills for their customers for a small fee? This sort of thing seems likely to get going and, since it has some of the appearance of paying interest on demand deposits, it may raise a question for the supervisory authorities.

If you can give me any light and leading on these questions, I would appreciate it.

With best regards.

Sincerely,

Allan

Letter to Alfred Hayes

June 26, 1960

Dear Al:

Thank you for letting me in on some of the thinking at the Bank on the question of interest rate ceilings, a confidence which I will respect, of course. I thought the memorandum read as if it were a joint product of Research and Bank Supervision, and that it had some of the virtues and some of the defects of such joint ventures.

Being footloose and fancy-free, I can wave my arms and raise my voice. I think the memorandum too readily accepts the role of operating within existing law and too easily kisses off market freedom. My own rampant view is that there is no longer necessity for having a government body at Washington fix ceilings on the rate of interest which can be paid by banks on time and savings deposits. In terms of asset quality, liquidity, and banks with less than adequate management, there is no comparison between 1930 and 1960. The problem of banks making speculative loans and illiquid investments, in order to be able to pay high rates of interest, to the extent that it persists, seems to be almost wholly a problem of small banks with weak management. Supervisory authority should be exerted to eradicate such weakness, or its results in bank assets, not to keep the whole banking system under wraps in order to protect the weakness of the few. The weak small banks are probably pockets of monopoly, anyway, hiding behind the sanctity of the small, independent bank. And they probably are carrying some of the costs of their commercial business and their demand deposits, by shortchanging their savings depositors. Eventually they will be wiped out by merger, branch banking, or holding company banking, and inability to survive in competition with other thrift institutions.

But the fact that we are not writing on a blank sheet of paper is not sufficient justification for the supervisory authorities to cling to a power which has outworn its usefulness, and which may have become positively dangerous to the health of the whole commercial banking system.

If this all-out approach is wrong, or impractical, the ideas about greater flexibility expressed in the memorandum certainly point in the right direction. But do they go far enough? Using the distinctions between fixed time and savings deposits, and their use by banks, developed in the memorandum, how would it be to match the characteristics of the two kinds of deposits and of bank portfolios with the performance of short- and long-term interest rates, to get the following pattern?

(a) The ceiling rate on savings deposits should be fixed largely on the basis of what banks can earn on long-term investments over time, rather than in relation to current rates of interest in the market, and changes in the ceiling should be made infrequently.

(b) The ceiling on fixed time deposits should be higher at times and at times lower than the ceiling on savings deposits, and should be changed more frequently. This could be more readily done than in the case of savings deposits, especially when rates are going down, because the rate on fixed time deposits is a negotiated rate.

(c) Ceilings should not fix rates and, therefore, should not try to follow market rates too closely.

Maybe this merely shows how complicated a logical solution of the problem of fixing ceiling rates by administrative regulation can become, and how administrative difficulties can multiply. But a rule such as we have, simple enough to be applied to all banks in all circumstances, is procrustean.

I am piping down so far as the payment of interest on demand deposits is concerned. I would still like to know, however, whether bank buying and selling of Treasury bills for customers, for a fee, as distinguished from repurchase arrangements, would have any merit.

With best regards.

Sincerely,

Allan

P.S. I liked your statement before Subcommittee Number 3 of the House Banking and Currency Committee for two reasons. I agreed with what you said and the way you said it, and I was warmed by the mention of my name.

Letter to Alfred Hayes

Bolinas sur Mer
July 18, 1966

Dear Al:

I am typing this by the shore with inferior materials and equipment, and it may not be my usual immaculate job. I am rushing into correspondence because I am wondering whether you are as distressed as I am about recent developments with respect to interest rates, and by the proposals which are being put forward to deal with the situation.

It was distressing to me, first, when the Administration perpetuated its wrongheaded attitude toward Federal Reserve policy by having Joe Fowler recommend to the Congress the fixing of interest rate ceilings on certain classes of time deposits at banks and savings and loan associations. It is hard for me to see why he should have picked up the ball that Patman's committee had to drop so recently unless, in addition to concern about the position of the savings and loan associations, there is a rankling resentment which harks back to the action of the Federal Reserve in increasing the discount rate and raising the ceilings on time deposit interest rates last December. I noted that, in his letter to Representative Ullman, the Secretary recalled "that the Administration opposed the action of the Federal Reserve last December", and that he also presses a weak claim that the Administration has not been remiss in striving for a "healthy balance of monetary and fiscal policy".

And now comes the action of the Board of Governors reducing to 5 percent the ceiling rate which can be paid by banks on so-called multiple maturity CDs which mature in 90 days or more, and 4 percent on such deposit instruments which mature in less than 90 days. This rapid response to Administration and Congressional pressure (as well as to the difficulties of the existing situation) is a descent into the bog of price fixing by ineffective inches. The descent is becoming like the United States involvement in Vietnam; the more we struggle to get out, the deeper we sink in.

The way we got into the present mess was by setting interest rate ceilings, by legislation and regulation, which banks can pay on time deposits, while an aggressive savings and loan industry, without such restraints, was using every available means to provoke a shift of bank deposits into the shares of such associations. And then, when the banks were unleashed, their retaliatory actions in trying to attract deposits from their nonbank competitors, and their rapacity in trying to steal deposits from one another—*as well as to obtain a measure of relief from the restraint being imposed upon them by Federal Reserve policy*—compounded the difficulties in a difficult situation. Whatever slight amelioration of the immediate political and economic pressures the latest action of the Board of Governors may obtain, I suggest it represents another step in the wrong direction.

I start with the proposition that our present practice of monetary management rests mainly on our ability to regulate the availability of reserves in a banking system based on the maintenance of fractional reserves against deposits. That is the fulcrum of our main lever. And I proceed with the belief that trying to fix (or peg) market rates of interest beyond use of the discount rate, by statute or regulation, is tricky, dangerous, and habit forming. Pegging market rates of interest and pegging market prices of Government securities are two of a kind. They are both incompatible with a properly functioning money and capital market and with the proper functioning of the Federal Reserve System.

With these premises, and recognizing that the present situation is complicated by short-term political and economic pressures which seem to demand some action, I think that the action should be geared to the control of reserves and not to further control of interest rates. In this context, I thought that the earlier action of the Board of Governors in raising reserve requirements on certain time deposits at certain banks moved in the right direction (even though it appeared to me to be based on some slippery legal logic and even though it apparently did nothing to appease the critics of the System).

If a uniform reserve requirement on all deposits at all banks could be legislated, so as to preserve the aggregate total and without seriously disrupting the affairs of individual banks, it would approach the ideal of a primary reserve requirement geared to the needs of monetary policy and management, instead of a requirement geared to the historical accident of reserves related to the assumed liquidity needs of different kinds of deposits at banks in different places. Such legislation isn't in the realm of the possible at present, of course. A lesser step in the appropriate long-term direction, which would also take account of the short-term problem, would be a gradual increase in the reserve required against time CDs to the level of reserves required against demand deposits.

It seems to me that the banks—and particularly the banks in New York City and some other large centers—have played a dangerous game since last December with the difference between reserve requirements for demand and time deposits. When I was at the Bank at that time, some of your economists told me that there are a lot of leaks in the "circular flow of money". But I can't get it out of my head that most of the large figure CD funds were in the banks as somebody's demand deposits before the CD business took hold. This would suggest that the banks, in rapidly raising the rates on their CDs since December 1965, were seeking not only to meet aggressive competition from the savings institutions, but also were avoiding in some measure the restrictive policy of the System by promoting a switch from demand to time deposits. Rapid and massive shifts of this sort can be disruptive of monetary management and unbridled competition for deposits doesn't necessarily mean that funds are flowing to the place where they can be used most effectively. The response of interest rates to the course of the economy and to Federal Reserve action in recent months seems to me to have been excessive. Rates appear to have been ratcheted upward by the action of the banks with respect to CD funds, apart from the pressures of monetary policy and market supply and demand.

Action such as I am playing with, of course, would recreate some questions of fair competition as between banks and the savings institutions, but that is a relatively minor matter so far as overall monetary policy is concerned. The answer to that problem should be sought in equity of treatment of the banks and the savings institutions with respect to reserve requirements, taxes, and other things by the governments which charter them, and not in the fixing of interest rates (ceilings) by the Federal Reserve, the Home Loan Bank Board, or anyone else.

I realize that there is a lot more that could be said about all of this, but I had become so interested that I had to get something on paper quickly in order to seek your calm view. Am I lost in a thicket, or are the banks and the System?

With all the best.

Sincerely,

Allan

P.S. This is a long letter, but I forbore mentioning sterling which I am sure is on your mind these days. Those who say that this is an interesting time to be alive usually have little responsibility for anything big, or they would not be so chipper.

Excerpt from *Coordination of Economic Policy*, a paper presented before a joint meeting of the American Finance Association and the American Economic Association on December 23, 1966. (The entire paper appears in the *Journal of Finance*, May 1967.)

Of special concern, also, in the monetary sphere is the unfortunate situation into which we have drifted in the fixing of ceiling rates which commercial banks, mutual savings banks, and savings and loan associations may pay on savings and time deposits or share holdings. Originally introduced to try to protect commercial banks from their presumed folly, the authority to fix such ceilings has been stretched to serve as a handmaiden to general monetary policy in bringing pressure to bear on commercial banks to restrict their lending, and as a yo-yo device to shift funds from one type of thrift institution to another in accordance with the ideas of the authorities as to who should get what. This is a heady but dangerous business.

The history of such regulation of maximum rates of interest to be paid on time and savings deposits of various kinds and maturities is a journey down a road paved with good intentions and bad practices. They were first used by commercial banks as an excuse for not paying depositors as high a rate of interest on such deposits as market conditions might have warranted. Later they became a halter on the commercial banks when the savings banks, and particularly the aggressive savings and loan associations, began luring away bank customers with offers of interest rates much higher than the banks were allowed to pay. This hot money was invested by the savings and loan associations largely in long-term mortgages, a hazardous proceeding. Then the banks were periodically let loose by a lifting of the ceiling on the rates they could pay, and they immediately tried to reverse the flow of funds by quickly moving their rates up to the new ceilings. Finally this upward ratcheting of rates got out of hand and the savings and loan associations were least able to compete profitably for new funds at the new rates. Funds flowed out of these associations, but not so much into the banks as into securities, open market paper, and Government and Government agency obligations. At this stage, all financial intermediaries were being ill served by the rate ceilings, but the plight of the savings and loan associations was such that special legislation was sought and obtained which authorized the Federal regulatory authorities to get together and to give a rate advantage, for the time being, to some of these institutions. These attempts to fix interest rates and to direct savings flows have helped cause some of the most rapid and disruptive shifts in rates and in savings flows that we have ever experienced. It is hard to see how market forces could have done a worse job. Now we have our hand in a pocketful of fish hooks and it is going to be impossible to get it out without pain and discomfort.

Chapter 6

Federal Reserve Structure and Monetary Policy

Allan Sproul, as might have been expected from his background, for the most part believed strongly in the existing structural organization of the Federal Reserve System—both internally (a regional federation with central supervision) and externally ("independent within the government but not independent from the government").

The present chapter begins with his statement to a Congressional subcommittee in 1952; it is the fullest and most complete exposition he ever made on the question of Federal Reserve "independence". Next is a paper entitled "Reflections of a Central Banker", presented in December 1955 before a joint meeting of the American Finance Association and the American Economic Association. Three 1958 letters follow, all related to his membership (and then his nonmembership) on the Commission on Money and Credit. The final paper is a communication to the Congressional Joint Economic Committee opposing much of the Commission on Money and Credit's final report.

Ironically, it was Sproul himself who was largely responsible for the creation of the Commission on Money and Credit in the first place. He concluded "Reflections of a Central Banker" in 1955 by calling for "a fresh and thorough examination of our existing banking and credit machinery and our money and capital markets". At that time he was still president of the Bank and the appeal struck a responsive chord in influential circles.

Slightly over a year later, now no longer president, he enlarged on the theme in a talk before the Economic Club of Detroit on February 18, 1957: "We have had a succession of relatively narrow official inquiries into this or that phase of our monetary arrangements and our fiscal and credit policies since the war, some of which were constructive and bore good fruit and some of which assumed the ritual character of the mating dance of the fiddler crab without apparent results. Now we need a broad study, or an inquiry by an objective panel of citizens, divorced from partisan public and special private interests, who will develop a comprehensive picture of the structure of our financial system and the ways in which it operates."

The Commission on Money and Credit produced his "broad study"— but not one, in his view, sufficiently "divorced from partisan public and special private interests". Although he had initially accepted an invitation to become a member of the Commission, he withdrew before it began its deliberations on the ground that too many of its members had been chosen because of their special interest point of view—thereby foreclosing the opportunity to get an objective report devoted primarily to the public interest.

When the Commission's report finally came out, in 1961, he opposed many of its recommendations and strongly communicated those views to the Congress (see below), despite the fact that his old friend Marriner Eccles had been a leading member of the Commission and one of its foremost spokesmen. This caused a temporary estrangement between the two that was not fully healed until the late sixties, when they once again found common cause in their shared opposition to American military involvement in Vietnam.

Statement from *Monetary Policy and Management of the Public Debt,* **Hearings before the Subcommittee on General Credit Control and Debt Management of the Joint Committee on the Economic Report, 1952.**

April 22, 1952

Honorable Wright Patman, Chairman
Subcommittee on General Credit Control and
Debt Management of the Joint Committee
on the Economic Report
House of Representatives
Washington 25, D.C.

Dear Mr. Patman:

In the course of the recent hearings of your committee there were certain recurring questions which were never definitely answered, so far as I know, and which perhaps cannot be definitely answered. Nevertheless, the fact that they were not answered or, perhaps, cannot be answered definitively and categorically, should not be taken to mean that they contain proof of argument by default or opposition.

I have in mind such questions as the following, which may not have been asked in exactly this form but contained this substance:

> Is not the argument for an "independent" Federal Reserve System a denial of our democratic ability to function properly through the legislative and executive branches of the Government?

> Why should monetary policy be treated differently from, say, foreign policy or defense policy, in terms of the administrative arrangements and relations with the Congress and the executive?

Hasn't the trend in all other countries been to "nationalize" the central banks where they were not already "nationalized" and to make them directly responsible to the "government" through the "Treasury"?

Does not the growing interest of governments in economic affairs, and their growing participation in such affairs, make this trend logical and necessary?

These are questions which compel thought and analysis, even though one may feel, as I do, that the right answer does not follow the lead of the questioning.

In the first place, I think it should be continuously borne in mind that whenever stress is placed upon the need for the "independence" of the Federal Reserve System it does not mean independence from the Government but independence within the Government. In performing its major task—the administration of monetary policy—the Federal Reserve System is an agency of the Congress set up in a special form to bear the responsibility for that particular task which constitutionally belongs to the legislative branch of the Government.

It is in no sense a denial of our democratic form of Government to have the Reserve System set up the way it is. It is rather an expression of the ability of our democratic powers to meet new or changing conditions. The Congress, as the sovereign power in this area, has developed a special means of performing a function with respect to which it has final authority, but which it cannot administer from day to day. The Congress has, of necessity, had to delegate some segments of its power to agencies of its own creation which, in turn, are responsible to it. The Federal Reserve System as one of these agencies attempts, as does the Congress itself, to maintain close relations with the executive branch of the Government, for the purpose of achieving a coherent and generally unified economic program. But that does not mean that physical merger of the Congress or its agencies with the executive branch of the Government is necessary or desirable.

It really takes us little way along the road to understanding to ask why monetary policy should be treated differently from foreign policy or defense policy in terms of administrative arrangements. The form of the question implies that here are matters (defense policy and foreign policy) of greater importance to the country than monetary policy which are administered by the executive branch of the Government, through the State Department and the Defense Department, and not by an independent agency. No one, of course, would want to enter into a footless argument about the relative importance of policy in these areas to the citizens of the country—they are all of vital importance. It may suggest a difference between them, however, to remember that the Federal Reserve is trying to help guide, regulate, and to some extent control the functioning of the private economy, and primarily the domestic economy, whereas foreign policy and military policy, while they affect our private and domestic affairs, deal largely with our relations with other countries and governments. It is in the general area of regulation of domestic economic affairs that the Congress has found repeated use for "independent" agencies.

The underlying question is whether it is better to have the legislative branch in full and final control of the purse and the money of the country, directly and through an agency responsible to it, or whether these matters should be turned over to the executive branch for administration along with most other governmental affairs. The Constitution, insofar as its language may be applied to present-day conditions, leaves this matter with the Congress. Wisdom and experience support this early separation of powers. Over the years and within our Constitutional framework, the people have preferred to keep all aspects of the money power as the prerogative of their duly elected representatives in the Congress. The temptation to tamper with money for temporary gain or narrow purpose is always present, and particularly in times of economic stress. The power to do so should be kept where it can be most readily observed and its abuse most quickly punished. That place is not under the protective wing of the chief executive or hidden in one of the big departments of the executive branch of the Government.

It may be instructive in this regard to compare the role of the Congress with respect to debt management with its role in relation to monetary policy during the past three or four decades. It is significant, I think, that the Congress, at frequent intervals, has conducted comprehensive and useful inquiries into the conduct of monetary policy by the Federal Reserve System. It has not made similar inquiries into debt management; even during the investigations of this committee, which have been most far-reaching, debt management has been considered only in its broadest aspects and, essentially, only when it has become intertwined with credit policy. Yet debt management is a concern of the Congress, particularly under present-day conditions. To be sure there are specific acts of the Congress which authorize whatever is done in the name of debt management, but the economic ramifications of the decisions taken with such legal authority are generally unobserved or unexamined. There seems to have been a gradual and more or less tacit acceptance of the assumption that debt management is a function of the executive branch of Government with which the Congress need not concern itself once it has passed the enabling legislation. That is what might happen to monetary policy if it became imbedded in the executive branch of the Government. That would, I think, be a disservice to the country. The inquiry of this committee, and other Congressional investigations which have preceded it, would seem to provide a clear-cut demonstration of the contributions which can be made to the nation's economic welfare by arrangements which lead the Congress to appraise performance of its own agent from time to time.

The particular forms and administrative arrangements which have worked in foreign countries for the administration of monetary policy are not a usable guide for us. In most such countries, of similar economic maturity and with similar economic systems, the "government" comprises both the executive and legislative branches in one responsible body or parliament. The executive must explain and justify policy from day to day, and is exposed to legislative questioning and the possibility of legislative repudiation without the protection of a fixed term of office. The trend of relationship in such countries between governments and central banks has been a process of evolution. No matter what their beginnings the central banks have evolved as "public" institutions. Changes from private ownership to public ownership, where they have occurred, have quite often confirmed what had already happened. They have been changes of form rather than of substance and have usually tended to perpetuate some independence (as I would define independence) for the central bank rather than to snuff it out.

It is more useful, as a guide, for us to observe that in most of these countries, and certainly in the economically more mature countries, central banking is regarded as a field requiring special technical competence and continuity of management rather than complete subordination to the government of the day. The head of the central bank in these countries is not brought directly into the government and does not necessarily change with changes in the government. The central bank is still a place where views on economic matters and monetary policy can be independently developed and candidly put forward no matter what the precise relations to the government may be. It is chiefly in the countries which are less advanced economically, where monetary policy is likely to be less developed, and where the central bank is primarily the fiscal agent of the government, that central bankers are political appointees responsible to and changing with each new executive.

I come back to the conclusion that neither our form of government nor the experience of foreign countries requires or recommends the placing of the Federal Reserve System in the executive branch of the Government. It is the pursuit of a doubtful logic and of neatness in administrative chart making which suggests this solution of our problem. The fact that there have been unfortunate differences of opinion between the Treasury and the Federal Reserve during recent years does not require the Congress to abandon its agent to the executive branch in order to bring about a better coordination of powers. It has already been pointed out that the Congress, through its specialized committees, reviews from time to time the manner in which the powers it has delegated to the Federal Reserve System are exercised. If, in the course of such reviews, the Congress finds that relationships between its delegated agent and the executive branch of the Government are not what it wishes them to be, it has remedies at hand. It can define more fully and more clearly what it expects these relationships to be, an approach which recommended itself to the Douglas Subcommittee of the Joint Committee on the Economic Report when it reviewed the problem.

On the basis of my experience which now comprises over thirty years in the Federal Reserve System at two Federal Reserve Banks, and attempting to make allowance for the bias which such long association can foster, I believe that the Federal Reserve System is an expression of an adaptable creative government. The System is by no means perfect; it needs improvement. But it can provide a competent mechanism, and a continuity of able personnel, which will enable us to cope with the day-to-day intricacies of monetary policy, while remaining responsive to the general economic purposes of the Government. The inquiry of your committee, and the Congressional investigations which have preceded it, provide a demonstration, I believe, of the advantages of continuing the existing direct relationship of the Federal Reserve System to the Congress, which causes the Congress to undertake periodic comprehensive appraisals of System performance.

If there is still time and if you think it would serve a useful purpose, I would like to have this statement added to my testimony before the committee.

Yours faithfully,

Allan Sproul

At the age of fourteen, in 1910.

High school yearbook editor, 1914.

Officers' training camp, in 1917.

Flying cadet, 1918.

Aboard the S.S. Europa, returning from Europe, in 1934: left to right,
George L. Harrison, head of the Federal Reserve Bank of New York;
Montagu C. Norman, governor of the Bank of England; Allan Sproul;
ship's captain, Oscar Scharff.

In London in 1949, with Rt.
Hon. Hugh Dalton (left),
Chancellor of the Exchequer,
and others.

Considerations Involved in Offer
of Presidency of World Bank.

1. Three important areas of financial operations to help attain economic stability and contribute to world peace.

   (a) To help promote maximum attainable degree of domestic economic stability — without stability in United States, stability in world is unlikely. I am already working in this field and an important period of development may now lie ahead. To shift now would be to plug one hole by creating another. Leave of absence from Federal Reserve Bank might be a compromise, but not fair to Reserve Bank.

   (b) To maintain maximum degree of stability in the foreign exchanges. This is a field in which central banks formerly played a part but it has now been taken over by the International Monetary Fund.

   (c) To assist in immediate reconstruction of foreign countries and to facilitate a steady and adequate flow of foreign investment in the future. This was formerly the field of direct government loans and of private international banking. World Bank now takes its place in this field — not one in which my main experience lies.

2. The organization of the World Bank is terrible at the highest levels. Minimum of twelve and a

maximum of twenty five executive directors
and alternates — full time — with not enough
to do. Policy and administration get badly mixed.
I don't like and am not good at this kind of
wrestling match.

3. Bank operations may well be more political (in broad
sense) than economic. United States will be the
big lender and the most powerful member. N.A.C.
directs the U.S. Executive Director. The President
as an international official is insulated from this
power center — any contact he has must
be informal and circumvented. The U.S.
Executive director is the direct representative of
the real power. I do not like and am not
too good at the sort of politics — economics
and politics — administration which seems
inevitable.

4. Personal — M.M.S. Upset at a bad time.
    Dislikes whole set up. Thinks it would
    be bad for me.
    — H.S. Approaching critical opportunity
    in life of F.R. system and would like
    to play out that string. To try & keep
    my hand in (leave of absence) and take on

    the stresses and strains of the world
    bank job would be beyond my physical
    capacity.

William McChesney Martin, Jr. (left), Chairman of the Board of Governors of the Federal Reserve System, and Allan Sproul, shortly after their testimony on "bills only" before a Congressional subcommittee in 1954.

Allan Sproul in the early 1950s.

Allan Sproul in 1960.

Paper read at joint meeting of American Finance Association and American Economic Association, New York City, December 29, 1955. Published in *Journal of Finance* (March 1956).

Reflections of a Central Banker

When you invite someone who is not a professional economist to speak on an occasion of this sort, there is always the danger that he will try to talk like a professional economist, and thus make a fool of himself while failing to fool his audience. I am not a professional economist. I hate to make a fool of myself. And I know I could not fool you.

I may have to skate pretty close to what is, for me, the thin ice of theoretical economics, however, because although I am not a professional economist I am a practitioner of an art which must draw inspiration from the work of professional economists. Central banking is largely practical economics, a sort of laggard son of theoretical economics, and I have been practicing central banking for the past thirty-five years. My long apprenticeship in the field is the excuse for the title which has been given to my talk, "Reflections of a Central Banker". Maybe that sounds as if I were going to give you some rocking-chair stories of my experience, but that is not my intention. I think it would be pretty dull. What I would like to do is to discuss a few of the things I have observed and thought about while I have been an officer of the Federal Reserve System, and which I think might merit a larger measure of interest and attention from you.

Monetary policy was in the doldrums for a number of years prior to and during World War II. It had been running fast before a brisk breeze for quite a while prior to that time, and then the wind died down and its sails went slack. Big claims had been made for it as a solvent of our economic ills, and when it couldn't support these claims there was a tendency to discard it in favor of more direct and what might seem to be more powerful economic controls. I suspect that somewhat the same pattern could be traced in the interest of economists, and particularly the younger economists, in the problems of central banking. For a time, preceding and following the passage of the Federal Reserve Act in 1913, such problems attracted a lot of men. Then it began to appear that more important work could be done, in other branches of economics, while interest in central banking suffered a relative decline. Now there has been something of a renaissance in the use of monetary policy as one of the means of achieving greater economic stability, without sacrificing too much economic freedom. If we are careful not to claim too much for it, it may hold its place. And I am hoping that central banking problems will similarly recapture the interest of a new generation of economists.

Let me speak first and most particularly about the Federal Reserve System, its organization, its policies, and its techniques. You all know the general organization of the System, but you may not all be aware of the evolutionary changes which have been taking place within the general organization. The main outlines of the System are much as they were when the System was established forty-one years ago: a regional system, federal in character, with a national coordinating and supervisory body at Washington and twelve regional Federal Reserve Banks which are the operating arms of the System in their respective districts.

Within this framework, however, there has been a definite tendency for power and influence to gravitate toward the center, a corollary of developments in other areas of social, political, and economic organization, as well as a result of growing familiarity at the center with the means of accomplishing things at the periphery. Fortunately, I think, for the development of the System and the good of the country this tendency has not gone so far as to destroy either the federal character of the System in terms of policy formation or its regional character in terms of policy execution.

That this is so is largely due to the development of the Federal Open Market Committee and its evolution as a body in which the various parts of the System are represented not by blocs, not by opposing groups of members of the Board of Governors on one side and presidents of Federal Reserve Banks on the other, but by individuals having equal authority and equal statutory responsibilities with respect to one of the most important functions of the System, namely, open market operations.

It is true that the means of credit control, other than open market operations, are scattered about the System in what seems to be an illogical manner. Discount rates are fixed by the board of directors of the individual Federal Reserve Banks, but are reviewed and determined by the Board of Governors, and the setting of reserve and margin requirements is wholly a charge of the Board of Governors. But all of these measures of credit control must be integrated and used as a common kit of tools. The Federal Open Market Committee provides the forum where discussion of their coordinated use can take place without unnecessarily infringing upon the rights and duties of other parts of the System. The illogical, in terms of organization charts and precisely drawn lines of authority, becomes logical in terms of the evolution of a body which appropriately and effectively represents all parts of the System.

It may be useful to recall how this unique arm of the System developed, not from some sudden inspirational attack on the problem of bringing national unity to a regional central banking system, but by trial and error during a shakedown cruise of about twenty years' duration. In the beginning, adjustments of the reserve positions of member banks were made entirely through the discount window. Early open market operations emerged in the form of an attempt by individual Federal Reserve Banks to supplement their earnings. It soon became apparent that the effect of these purchases and sales of Government securities (and bankers' bills) was to put reserves into the banking system or to take them out without regard for what might be credit policy at the time. The first informal attempt to correct the situation was the adoption by the Conference of Governors (presidents now) of Federal Reserve Banks, in 1922, of a policy of buying and selling Government obligations in an orderly and systematic manner, and the appointment of a committee of five governors to see that this was done. This loose arrangement was tightened up somewhat by the Federal Reserve Board in 1923, and the rule was adopted, which has since become a statutory principle of open market operations, that the time, character, and volume of such operations must be governed with primary regard to the accommodation of commerce and business and to their effect on the general credit situation. In 1930 an open market policy conference was created which included a representative of each of the twelve Federal Reserve Banks. Statutory recognition of and restraint upon this particular method of conducting open market operations was legislated in 1933, when the banking act of that year created a Federal Open Market Committee and prohibited open market operations of Federal Reserve Banks except in accordance with the regulations of the Federal Reserve Board. The Federal Open Market Committee in its present form came into being with the passage of the Banking Act of 1935, which also made it mandatory for Federal Reserve Banks to engage in open market operations in accordance with the directions and regulations of the Committee.

So far so good. Evolution has proceeded by a process of natural selection toward a higher form of organism, which retains some of the desirable characteristics of regional organization within a federal system, while acquiring the powers necessary to a coordination of national policy under present-day conditions. This organism has survived for twenty years and given evidence of being able to adapt itself to environmental change.

There are those, however, who see in the persistence of present regional representation on the Federal Open Market Committee a serious flaw in our credit control machinery. They appear to believe that this has enabled the poachers to remain on the Committee along with the game wardens, in the person of the five presidents of Federal Reserve Banks who are members of the Committee along with the seven members of the Board of Governors. The presidents of the Federal Reserve Banks, they say, are selected by the directors of the banks—to be sure, with the approval of the Board of Governors. The nine men who serve as directors of Federal Reserve Banks include six men elected by the member banks of their District, and three of these men are bankers. Ergo, the presidents of Federal Reserve Banks are the representatives of the member banks and, in political terms, must be responsive to the wishes of their constituents or they won't be presidents very long. And so, it is claimed, the group which is supposed to be regulated and controlled has at least five fingers in the pie.

This line of chain reasoning has its appeal if you believe that the presidents of Federal Reserve Banks are so beholden to commercial bankers for their jobs, and so lacking in awareness of their statutory responsibilities that they cannot honestly serve the public interest as members of the Federal Open Market Committee. The fact is, however, that the relation between a president of a Federal Reserve Bank and the bankers of his District is not that of an elected representative and his constituents or an employee and his employer. The present somewhat complicated arrangements for the election and appointment of directors of Federal Reserve Banks, and for the appointment of presidents of Federal Reserve Banks by these directors, have instead a double virtue. First, they inject into the System's conduct of its everyday affairs the standards of efficiency and practical judgment that well-chosen business executives can provide from their own experience—and that includes everything from judging the fitness of a man to administer the complex operations of a Federal Reserve Bank to the maintenance of its plant and equipment. This has contributed to an operating performance which has protected Federal Reserve Banks from much of the criticism which is leveled against other institutions not prodded toward efficiency by the profit motive. Second, these electoral arrangements keep the presidents of Federal Reserve Banks directly in touch with men who are aware of banking and credit conditions and economic developments in their Districts, and who can help to interpret credit policy to the banking, business, and agricultural community, without making the presidents subservient to whatever may be the selfish interests of any group in the community.

On the even more important level of policy formation, the problem is not comparable to that faced by a government regulatory body fixing rates and conditions of service under monopoly or semimonopoly conditions, nor to the problem of an administrative tribunal watching over observance of the law. The main problem of the central banking system is the appraisal of major developments affecting the whole economy and the formulation of a policy which will influence the money and credit sector of that economy so as to contribute to the stability of the economy as a whole. This is a public service which requires of its practitioners continuous contact with economic processes, and with people in the marketplaces of the country as well as with the representatives of government at its political center. It requires practitioners with an awareness of the problems of an economy which is neither wholly private nor wholly public in character. It requires practitioners who are insulated against narrow partisan political influence on the one hand, and against narrow selfish private influence on the other, but who are responsive both to broad government policies and to the importance of private initiative and private enterprise in giving support to those policies. In my view there has been developed in the Federal Reserve System in general, and in the Federal Open Market Committee in particular, a unique contribution to the democratic administration of such a task. There is no conflict of interest in this administration.

I have spoken of this matter of organization at some length because I think it is vital to the preservation of a Federal Reserve System which retains regional vigor in a national setting, and because attempts to destroy the Federal Open Market Committee, as presently constituted, have been made from time to time. In fact, a bill has been resting in a Congressional committee for the past year, which would abolish the Federal Open Market Committee and transfer its functions to an enlarged Board of Governors of the Federal Reserve System. That way lies a revolution in the organization of our credit control machinery. I believe that this is a question which goes well beyond the mere mechanics of organization, and which needs and deserves your closest scrutiny as citizens, as well as economists and men of finance.

So much for organization. Now for reference to policies. The preamble to the Federal Reserve Act says that the Federal Reserve System is to be concerned with the provision of an elastic currency, affording a means of rediscounting commercial paper, and establishing a more effective supervision of banking in the United States, and for other purposes. Well, the "other purposes" have long since stolen the show, as must be the case when the manifold objects of an economic experiment are compressed into a few words, no matter how well chosen. We are all now engaged in an attempt to prevent the occurrence of wide and deep economic fluctuations and to mitigate the hardships of the smaller cyclical functions and the necessary internal adjustments of a dynamic, growing, relatively free-choice economy.

The role of the central banking system in this attempt to achieve better balance in our economy has never been spelled out specifically, and probably cannot be. We were not specifically mentioned in the Employment Act of 1946, which gave expression to the present general concept of the economic role of government, but our share of the general responsibility derives largely from that expression of national policy. I have always felt, however, that if we are to be true to the explicit requirements of our own charter we must emphasize the implicit requirements of this broader charter by combining stability of the purchasing power of the dollar with the promotion of the most effective possible utilization of our resources. We must be alert to oppose both inflationary and deflationary pressures, either one of which can upset the precarious balance of a high-employment, high-production, high-income economy.

We are pretty much all of one mind, I take it, when it comes to opposing deflationary forces which threaten a waste of human and material resources. But there is no such unanimity when inflation—usually trotted out as mild inflation—is in prospect or in being. Here is a central banking problem with respect to which we should, perhaps, have had more help from you than you have so far given us. Are we right in the belief that stability of the dollar and a growing high-level economy are compatible? Or, at least, are we right in our belief that there are so many forces in the economy which now exert inflationary pressures as to make it likely that our role will generally be to resist those pressures in the interest of sustained economic growth? The siren song of gradual modest inflation, if it be that and not the music of the spheres, appeals to many groups, political and economic. There is a tendency to relax and enjoy the sound of more money in the cash register and the appearance of more dollars in the balance sheet and in the pay envelope. The problem has become a fundamental one in the administration of monetary policy, and your advice and counsel and, indeed, your leadership are needed.

There are those, of course, who think the answer has already been given, and that our powers have been reduced to exerting a gentle tug on the reins from time to time, which is really administered by the horse. With that I cannot agree; I cannot bear witness to the impotence of our central banking system. It still has considerable power, even though we recognize, as I think we must, that general monetary controls can no longer be used so drastically as to bring about a severe restriction of the money supply with restriction of income, production, and employment in its wake. In this we would only find support if we were faced with a runaway inflation due solely or primarily to monetary causes. That is an emergency we have not had to face, and certainly do not have any desire to face, even though the actual experience of such a catastrophe might subsequently make for broader public understanding of the anti-inflationary steps we must take from time to time. In developed countries which have experienced hyper-inflation the central bank has only to mention the word "inflation" to bring a large measure of public support to a restrictive credit policy. When we mention inflation as a reason for trying to restrain a boom, which shows signs of temporarily exhausting physical capacity to increase the supply of goods and services, and in circumstances when further injections of bank credit are likely to show up largely if not entirely in increased prices, we are apt to be charged with crying wolf when there is no wolf, to be denounced as apostles of deflation. And, if actual inflation does not develop, perhaps because we have done our job of helping curb its development, the accusation against us seems to gain increased validity. You can see why I would like to have aid and comfort in resolving doubts about our ability to combine a stable dollar with a growing, expanding, high-level, peacetime economy.

Another aspect of policy formation which concerns me is whether or not undue reliance is now being placed upon the judgments of men, and whether we should seek some automatic or mechanical guides to policy action. I do not think that we have been led too far astray by reading our press clippings. When it is said of the Federal Open Market Committee that "these twelve men have more financial power than any other official body in United States history", we may think it will impress our children and grandchildren, but we are also humble enough to recognize that the power we wield is a circumscribed one which cannot be wielded arbitrarily or capriciously. In the first place, it is a power exercised by a group of individuals of differing backgrounds and talents, and with differing approaches to the policy actions upon which they must finally agree. There are checks and balances such as are characteristic of our whole concept of government, which give assurance that decisions will be reached by a deliberate process, and that power will not be wielded by an individual who might acquire the habits of a despot. In the second place, it is power exercised in the white light of full disclosure: weekly, monthly, and annually our actions are publicly reported for all to examine and to judge. Finally, it is power exercised within the limits of national objectives and public tolerance, which would not permit the Committee to indulge a sense of power or to experiment rashly with it, even if it were so inclined.

But to recognize the limitations of our powers is not to deny their importance. We must and do take them very seriously. We realize that we are trying to measure and adjust the flow of credit in a money economy, and we are steeped in the belief that whether the economy works well or poorly depends in part on our success or failure in discharging our responsibilities. And therein, I think, lies a danger. The oppressive character of such a heavy responsibility leads men to seek some automatic or mechanical device as a guide to policy action, in order to remove the risk of exercising fallible human judgment. The gold standard, as it existed during the latter part of the nineteenth century and the early years of the present century, largely performed this role in those countries which had central banks and which looked first and almost entirely to the state of their balance of payments and the size of their gold reserves in formulating central bank policy.

Those "good old days" began to pass into history, however, when central bankers began consciously to interfere with the effects of inflows and outflows of gold upon the domestic credit situation and, through it, upon the domestic economy. They receded further into limbo as national policy became more and more oriented toward the maintenance of high levels of production and employment at home, and tried to fit together the international and the domestic situation without subordinating one to the other.

And yet there have been and no doubt are serious students of central banking who believe that it cannot function properly without a "norm" of behavior, or a mathematical equation, which will tell its human guides what to do and when to do it. In the present state of our knowledge of the functioning of the economic world, and despite the flood of available statistics which never seems to be out of spate, I do not believe that we can now devise a "norm" or an equation which will relieve us in any substantial and consistent way of the necessity of exercising human judgment in discharging our responsibilities. What we need is not just a catalogue and synthesis of symptoms, but an appraisal of a whole situation, including the complex reactions of human beings—businessmen, labor leaders, consumers, politicians. Early in my career in the Federal Reserve System I read a statement by Allyn Young which impressed me then and impresses me now:

> *In fact, we can be certain that reliance upon any simple rule or set of rules would be dangerous. Economic situations are never twice alike. They are compounded of different elements—foreign and domestic, agricultural and industrial, monetary and non-monetary, psychological and physical—and these various elements are combined in constantly shifting proportions.*
>
> *"Scientific" analysis, unaided, can never carry the inquirer to the heart of an economic situation. Judgment and wisdom—the power to take a complex set of considerations into account and come to a balanced view of them—are quite as much needed as facts and theories. The Federal Reserve System needs to operate in the light of all the information it can get, and it*

needs to have this information organized and analyzed in such a way as to give the maximum amount of illumination. But it also needs the guidance of that practical wisdom which is born only of experience.

If in our time, however, with increasing knowledge of how credit policy works, we can discover a "norm" of action, or a mathematical guide to policy, our task would be greatly simplified. To do that, we shall have to know more than we yet know about how monetary and credit policy actually affect the economy as a whole and in its various parts, and with what leads and lags. This will mean deep probing into the operations of our money and banking system as it is now constituted, and into the effects of changes of monetary and credit policy upon the whole economy working through the banking system. Until this job is further along, a good motto for central banks may continue to be the lines of the poet:

Our stability is but balance
And wisdom lies in masterful
Administration of the unforeseen.

I am now going to turn to one of the techniques of execution of central bank policy, partly because it has importance from a general economic standpoint which transcends its purely technical trappings, and partly because it has been the subject of some public comment and discussion during the past year or two. I refer to the range of open market operations: whether such operations should be rigidly confined to short-term Government securities except under the most unusual circumstances or whether a willingness at times to operate over the whole range of maturities of Government obligations would provide a better means of making credit policy effective. I am not going to reiterate all of my own views which are already in the record and which are distinctly minority views within the Federal Open Market Committee. There are as yet no absolutes in this business, however. Those who advocate, and I who oppose, the present techniques of the Federal Open Market Committee are merely climbing the hill on opposite sides, trying to reach the same summit of knowledge and effectiveness.

But I do think that the question is one worthy of the attention of at least some of you who are here today, not merely as a matter of casual comment in panel discussions, or writings on other subjects, but as something which has real economic significance and deserves serious study. And I am encouraged in this opinion by the articles which have appeared in the journals during the past year. If the present technique derives from a too rigid application of supposed classical economics to problems of money and credit, we need enlightenment from you.

I had supposed that the classical economists, the men of private property and free markets, did not think that free markets could provide everything necessary to the public good, and that if they were our contemporaries they might have thought of the market for money and credit as something separate and apart from other markets, and as an appropriate area of intervention by government or agencies of government—intervention at that cross-section of the economy where the public need for some overall economic guidance toward stability could be provided with a minimum of direct intrusion into the details of production and distribution. And I had supposed that this would mean central bank action to help the market in determining the significant characteristics of the maturity structure of interest rates implied by the kind of credit policy being pursued—not to try to set decimal points on daily quotations, nor to peg a curve, but to nudge the market in the direction sought by credit policy. And finally I had supposed that the effects of increases or decreases in capital values, arising from changes in long-term rates of interest, were becoming more and more important in an economy in which public as well as private debts have become so large a part of our so-called assets, and that some direct intervention in this area might at times be appropriate. Whether or not these or contrary suppositions are true, it seems to me that this matter of open market techniques involves problems of economic significance beyond its immediate technical application, and that it deserves your study and your published findings.

There is another area of credit administration which can be brought under the loose heading of techniques. That is the problem of selective credit controls, and particularly the control of consumer instalment credit. I suppose that all of us who have a bias against detailed planning "from above" would prefer that credit policy accomplish its major aims by general quantitative controls which work impersonally but pervasively, and without interfering directly with individual transactions. But if there has grown up a form of credit extension which, no matter how prodigious its contribution to mass production and mass consumption, is also introducing a dangerous element of instability in our economy, and if it is difficult to reach this credit area by general credit measures without adversely affecting all of the less avid users of credit, is there not a case for a selective credit control? Thackeray says in *Vanity Fair*: "Everybody must have observed how well those live who are comfortably and thoroughly in debt; how they deny themselves nothing; how jolly and easy they are in their minds."

Well, I am not jolly and easy in my mind. I am disturbed by the present situation in consumer instalment credit, just as I was concerned, under different conditions and for different reasons, about stock market credit until the Board of Governors was given power to establish, and to vary, margin requirements. I am disturbed not by the total amount of consumer credit, but by the fact or the indication that successive relaxation of terms has been largely responsible for keeping the ball in the air. This is a process which cannot go on indefinitely, and when it ceases there will come a time when repayment of old debt will catch up with new extensions of credit. The special stimulus of a rapidly increasing net supply of consumer credit, which has contributed so much to the record production and distribution of consumer durable goods during the past year, will then be gone, at least temporarily. Will it then become clear that we drove our productive capacity to unsustainable limits—for the present—by borrowing consumer demand from the future?

This is a subject on which many voices have expressed many views, but usually they have not been views which seemed objective enough to help resolve the question in the best interest of society as a whole. I know that there are those who believe that selective credit controls are a dangerous step on the road to general overall planning, and I have no desire to become a fellow traveler on that road. But I do believe that there is a temptation to abuse consumer credit in boom times, that it can thus become a serious source of instability in our economy, and that we would not jeopardize our general freedom from direct controls by giving the Federal Reserve System permanent authority to regulate consumer credit. I freely admit, however, that this view would be better held if it were based more firmly on objective study and research into the place of consumer credit in our economy and less on observation and opinion. That is the sort of basis for consideration and action which you could provide.

The same or something similar might be said of mortgage financing, but I shall not try to go into that. Economics and social objectives become intermingled so fiercely when housing is discussed as to make calmness and objectivity a handicap, if not a badge of moral delinquency.

The basic question involved in both cases is whether an attempt should be made through regulation of these specific types of credit to exert a stabilizing influence on areas of the economy which, in the past, appear to have been major sources of instability of employment and production, or whether we should be content with efforts to regulate the overall availability and cost of credit, hoping that fluctuations in the major areas of the economy will balance out. Our experience thus far suggests to me that general credit controls can exert an effective influence on these particular types of credit only with a considerable lag, and that we cannot rely upon countervailing forces in the economy to maintain overall stability.

Perhaps you can see where I have been heading in these somewhat random remarks, which have touched on a few aspects of central banking organization, policies, and techniques, while not mentioning others of equal or, perhaps, even greater importance. In general my purpose has been to frame a plea for help—a plea that theoretical economics come more steadily and effectively to the aid of practical economics in such fields as central banking.

I recognize that theoretical economics is the basis of practical economics. And I recognize that theoretical economists, in our time, seem mostly to have preferred to work on general principles, or on building models of economic performance, rather than on economic policies and their effects. I have not the competence to challenge the value of their work, but I question whether it is enough. I question whether economists individually and as a group can fulfill their obligations as citizens, as well as students and scholars, if they do not try to bring these interests together. I would say we need a revival of political economy, and I would invite you to look on central banking as a good place to start. The economists of an earlier day did not hesitate to jump into the thick of battle over current issues, and it did not seem to lower their academic standing then nor should it now. They were pamphleteers, they organized and participated in public meetings and discussion groups, they brought their influence to bear in any way they could on public officials and private citizens. They were pungent and provocative in debate. Macaulay said of James Mill and his followers on one occasion, "These smatterers whose attainments just suffice to elevate them from the insignificance of dunces to the dignity of bores." Perhaps that sort of thing is a little too violent for our present mood and condition. But it might be better than withdrawing completely into a realm of esoteric jargon, or indulging in an excess of politeness in dealing with your peers and your public, so that issues are seldom drawn clearly enough to attract public attention and promote public understanding. By your studies and your research and your application to the problems of economic theory, you have earned the right to be heard, and to give some sense of continuing direction to official action and to public opinion. I would like to see that right more vigorously exercised.

I feel that it could be exercised more vigorously and to advantage in the field of central banking. We have excellent research staffs in the Federal Reserve System: able economists and statisticians and devoted students of money and banking problems. But their work needs more cross-fertilization and critical analysis by thoughtful and disciplined minds outside the System who can apply their talents to this special field without the bias of an organizational viewpoint. Not enough work has been done, I would say, on the monetary problems of a mixed government-private economy, on the functioning and form of a fractional reserve banking system in such an economy, on the growing importance of other financial institutions, which crisscross both the fields of commercial banking and investment banking, and on the performance and characteristics of our money and capital markets. These are subjects which are becoming critical in the development of central banking.

You have tended, I venture to say, to occupy yourselves too much with the refinement of old ideas which are no longer wholly relevant, with the cataloguing of new economic processes, with the application of mathematical equations to situations too dependent on human behavior to be amenable to such treatment, or with building utopian models of the dream world of the future, while neglecting the hard but rewarding task of studying the present in a way which would contribute effectively to public policy and private well-being. If you will not use it against me, I would say that you have left the latter task to the improvised judgments of practitioners who have lacked the time or the equipment needed to work out a coherent and consistent basis for the actions which they must take.

It is said that there has been a renaissance of monetary and credit policy in recent years. In fact, some extravagant claims are again beginning to appear concerning the power and influence of monetary measures in curing or ameliorating our economic ills. Governments may be tempted to commit or condone economic errors, in the hope that monetary policy can redress the balance, and in the hope that the central banking system will stand as a buffer between the government and an electorate which chafes at restraint. We shall have to guard against asking too much of monetary policy. But it is a fact that monetary measures have reestablished themselves, and rightly so, as one of the principal means used by governments to try to keep national economies in order without the stifling restrictions of more direct physical controls.

What I would now like to see is a renaissance in the study of money and banking in general and of central banking in particular. I would like to see a fresh and thorough examination of our existing banking and credit machinery and our money and capital markets. I would hope that out of such study and examination would come new ideas and new proposals which would give shape and direction to future public policies and private actions. It would be a task worthy of the best talent you can bring to bear on it.

Letter to Alfred Hayes

February 21, 1958

Dear Al:

I want you to know that I have been asked and have agreed to serve as a member of the Commission on Money and Credit which is being set up by the Committee for Economic Development, with the financial support of the Ford Foundation. Although I consider this commission distinctly second best, as compared with a commission which might have been named by the President, if the Congress had been so inclined, I practically chiseled out the niche in which I have been placed. It would have been difficult for me to decline to serve, even if I had wished to do so, and I had no such wish. I think this way of attacking the problems involved is better than not attacking them at all, or attacking them piecemeal.

The personnel of the Commission is not going to be what I would have considered ideal, either; that is, a group of men with sufficient general knowledge of the field to enable them to use "experts" wisely, and sufficiently objective to be able to hear and consider all points of view, and to determine whether and to what extent differing points of view should be reflected in the findings of the Commission and its recommendations for action. This was never a realistic hope, I suppose, and it may not even have been a good idea. Whether it was or not, the Commission is to be made up of people representative of different interests and different geographical areas—big business, small business, big banks, small banks, other financial institutions, labor, agriculture, etc., coming from the northeast, the southeast, the middle west, the far west, etc. I shall now have to hope that the members of the Commission do not consider themselves as having been selected to "represent" these various interests and places, in the sense of being bound to support the views and interests of their "constituents", whether they serve the broad national interest or not. Who knows, maybe my colleagues on the Commission will prove to be as objective as I think I am!

As you know, the studies of the Commission are to go forward during the three years ending December 31, 1960, and it is anticipated that the Commission will meet, on the average, about once a month and will have lots of homework, too. No doubt the Federal Reserve System will be called upon to help the Commission in many ways. As an individual member of the Commission, I shall also need help, and I hope that I can call upon the people at the New York Bank from time to time, if I am not too greedy in my calls. This would be a happy arrangement for me if it is agreeable to you.

I was interested, of course, in the announcement Wednesday afternoon that the Board of Governors had reduced the reserve requirements of member banks. It had seemed to me, with the sharp deepening of the recession, the System was being a little niggardly in increasing the reserves of the banks through open market operations, even though the effect of the actions it has taken has been dramatic in terms of the interest rate structure. It now looks as if, following the pattern of last November when open market action was preceded by discount rate action, the System has taken action on reserve requirements rather than through the more gradual processes of the open market. This has the advantage of bringing moves toward credit ease quickly to the attention of a much wider public, I suppose, than would open market operations. And this first homeopathic dose probably comforts a Board which is still worrying about a revival of inflationary pressures, and convinced it erred in 1953 when a massive dose of new reserves was administered.

On the well-established principle that economic situations are never twice alike, however, I am wondering whether the lesson the Board sees in 1953 can be applied in 1958. There is an equal danger, I think, that this recession is not 1953-54 (or 1948-49) over again, but a downturn which contains a much greater risk of going deeper and lasting longer than the two preceding postwar recessions. If this be so, it will be possible to wait too long to take more vigorous credit action, and we may then find that our medicine doesn't work as well as it might have earlier. It can be said that a tax cut will do the job if more vigorous action is needed, but I would like to have credit policy play its proper role, too. Nor am I convinced that we can turn the economic spigot on and off by fiscal means, as easily as now seems to be assumed; certainly not without inflationary risks which equal, if they do not exceed, those which might attend a more vigorous relaxation of credit.

The banks out here are disappointed, of course, in the small size of the reduction in reserve requirements. The amount of the immediate reduction for individual banks seems to them to be picayune, and bankers never have been much impressed by the effect of such a reduction on the lending and investing power of the whole banking system, even when they have understood it. They want something which enables them directly and immediately to increase their earning assets substantially. This latest move, therefore, is getting less credit than it deserves. (It leaves the Federal Reserve Bank of San Francisco further out on the limb; a case of misplaced independence which I believe must have been forced on Hermann Mengels by his directors.)

I hope that you don't mind my writing you in this way. I stay away from the San Francisco Bank, but I don't do so well when it comes to the New York Bank.

With best regards.

Sincerely,

Allan

Letter to Alfred Hayes

March 20, 1958

Dear Al:

Thank you for letting me know about the rumors which are going around about CED's Commission on Money and Credit. They had not reached me (nor had any direct information from headquarters), but I am not surprised and I suspect that they are true. It is now over a month since Don David telephoned me and then wrote me, asking me if I would serve as a member of the Commission. At that time I think he expected to be able to announce the membership of the Commission on or about March 1, a hope later deferred to mid-March. The delay in making the announcement had led me to wonder whether some of those invited were not willing to serve, and the labor people (two of them) would seem to be the most likely candidates.

This reminds me of our conversation, when I last saw you, about trying to get representatives of labor interested in Federal Reserve policies and operations. I told you, I think, of my failure to get anywhere with them, and expressed the hope that you would be more successful. Their suspicion of bankers (Wall Street?) is deep-seated and uninformed, and the more dangerous for that reason. It is time they realized that, if they are going to live and work in a money economy, they should know more about how such an economy works and should be eager to take part in attempts to improve its workings. I can't believe that they really want to do away with the private sector of our financial machinery.

I do come back, however, to the mistake which I think CED made in trying to have the membership of the Commission representative of various economic and geographical areas of the community. My idea was to have a commission which would carry its own credentials of competence in the field, and which would rely on its studies and hearings to bring out all points of view. I can't say that CED came close to this ideal in its proposed Commission (so far as I have had names), and some of those proposed really surprised me, and caused me to have second thoughts about serving. I still cling to the hope that a good job will be done, but not with the enthusiasm I once had. I try to remember, too, that I am inclined to think that my way of doing things is best!

With best wishes.

Sincerely,

Allan

Letter to Alfred Hayes

June 13, 1958

Dear Al:

I think that you should know that I have decided to withdraw from the Monetary Commission, and have so advised Don David.

The original prospectus of the Commission said that "It is of the utmost importance that the members of the Commission be persons of unquestioned reputation for competence and objectivity. The members should be chosen for their individual qualities, not as representatives of organizations or sectors of the community. A balanced representation of philosophies and approaches should be sought."

The Commission of fifteen members, on which I agreed to serve last February, did not wholly realize these ideals but came close enough, I thought, to make my membership useful and rewarding. The enlarged Commission, the membership of which was unknown to me until the CED press release came out at the end of May, departs so far from these ideals as to make my membership unpalatable. It comes down to a personal judgment as to the conditions and circumstances under which you can do your best work and hope for the satisfactions which a workman requires. I decided that I could not hope to find these conditions and circumstances as a member of this mixed and unwieldy Commission. It has been a tough decision for me to make. I have tried to make it calmly and without rancor.

Now that I am home again, there are many things I would like to talk over with you, which we didn't have time to get into when I was at the Bank. I think that my visits have been too hurried, but that I may write oftener to share ideas and views with you.

With best regards.

Sincerely,

Allan

From *Review of the Report of the Commission on Money and Credit*, **Hearings before the Joint Economic Committee, August 1961**

August 16, 1961

Honorable Wright Patman, Chairman
Joint Committee on the Economic Report
United States Congress
Washington, D.C.

Dear Mr. Patman:

I regret that I could not accept your invitation to appear at the current hearings of the Joint Committee on the Economic Report, to testify regarding the recommendations of the Commission on Money and Credit concerning the structure of the Federal Reserve System. I realize that a memorandum of views is not a wholly satisfactory substitute for an appearance before the Committee, with its opportunity for questioning by interested Committee members. Nevertheless, since the subject is one in which I have a keen interest, and a degree of knowledge based on thirty six years spent in the Federal Reserve System, I have thought it worthwhile to use this means of placing my views before the Joint Committee.

To identify myself in the manner which has become customary at hearings of the Committee, my name is Allan Sproul. I am a director of the Wells Fargo Bank and American Trust Company of San Francisco and of the Kaiser Aluminum and Chemical Corporation of Oakland, California, and I was president of the Federal Reserve Bank of New York and vice chairman of the Federal Open Market Committee for fifteen years from 1941 to 1956. In presenting my views, however, I represent no one but myself; neither the private business community, the commercial banks, nor my former associates in the Federal Reserve System.

I should also mention, I think, that I was named as a member of the Commission on Money and Credit when it was first being organized in February 1958. In preceding years I had been among those who had advocated a study of our financial system by a national monetary commission established by the government, and composed of a small number of men competent in the field, experienced in economic matters, and with a reputation for objectivity. This official or government commission did not come to pass. As a second choice, the private commission sponsored by the Committee for Economic Development seemed to offer a partially satisfactory means of bringing our financial machinery under scrutiny and suggesting possible ways of improving it. When I accepted appointment to the Commission in February 1958 it was to be a Commission of fifteen members "chosen for their individual qualities, not as representatives of organizations or sections of the community" with a "balanced representation of philosophical approaches". In mid-April 1958 I was advised that it had been decided that "for more ideal balance the Commission should be expanded to a minimum of twenty-five, bringing about representation of areas, points of view, and interests which were not adequately provided for in the Commission of fifteen as originally planned". I learned of the membership of the enlarged Commission by way of a press release on May 29, 1958. On June 12, 1958 I withdrew from the Commission. My resignation was announced in a press release of the Commission on January 22, 1959.

So much for identification. As you requested, I now address myself to that part of the recently published report of the Commission on Money and Credit (CMC), which has to do directly with the structure of the Federal Reserve System. In this area, at least, I suggest that the CMC, in its efforts to compromise the various points of view and interests of its members, produced a doubtful package of recommendations. Some of them are good but, in the aggregate, they represent an attempt to pacify those who would "nationalize"[1] the Federal Reserve System by destroying its Federal character, and they tend to water down the symbols of support of the System by the private financial community

[1] A vague general term used to frighten conservatives.

to the point of poisoning rather than preserving a relationship which has made successful evolutionary progress for half a century. I directly challenge, therefore, so far as the structure of the Federal Reserve System is concerned, the statement of the CMC in the introduction of its report, that it has tried to "confine its recommendations and suggestions for change only to situations where the present structure has not worked well".

What are the recommendations and suggestions of the CMC for changes in the structure of the Federal Reserve System?

1. The FRB (Board of Governors of the Federal Reserve System) Chairman and Vice Chairman should be designated by the President from among the Board's membership, to serve for four-year terms coterminous with the President's.

2. The FRB should consist of five members with overlapping ten-year terms, one expiring each odd-numbered year; members should be eligible for reappointment.

3. The FRB Chairman should be the chief executive officer of the Board, empowered to handle administrative matters. The law should be clarified to authorize the Board to delegate to Board committees or to Board members individually, or to senior staff officers of the Board, any of its functions in the administration of its powers in regard to the supervision of the banking structure, etc. Any actions so delegated should be subject to review in the Board's discretion.

4. Occupational and geographical qualifications for Board members should be eliminated. Instead, the statute should stipulate that members should be positively qualified by experience or education, competence, independence, and objectivity commensurate with the increased responsibilities recommended for them in the achievement of low levels of unemployment, an adequate rate of economic growth, and reasonable stability of price levels in the economy. Salaries of top officials throughout the Government

should be sharply increased and, in view of the gravity of their responsibilities, FRB members should be compensated at the highest salary level available for appointive offices in the Government.

5. The present statutory Federal Advisory Council should be replaced by an advisory council of twelve members appointed by the Board from nominees presented by the boards of directors of the Federal Reserve Banks, etc.

6. The law should formally constitute the twelve Federal Reserve Bank presidents as a conference of Federal Reserve Bank presidents, to meet at least four times a year with the Board, and oftener as the Board finds necessary.

7. The determination of open market policies should be vested in the Board. In establishing its open market policy, the Board should be required to consult with the twelve Federal Reserve Bank presidents. The determination of the rediscount rate (the same for all Reserve Banks) should be vested with the Board. In establishing this rate, the Board should be required to consult with the twelve Federal Reserve Bank presidents. The determination of reserve requirements should continue to be vested in the Board. In establishing these requirements, the Board should be required to consult with the twelve Federal Reserve Bank presidents.[2]

The first five of these recommendations, which I would characterize as the trimmings of this section of the report of the CMC, might be accepted, I think, as moves in the right direction.

The suggestion that the terms of office of the Chairman and Vice Chairman of the Board be made coterminous with the term of office of the President has been attacked by those who see this as an attempt to introduce partisan politics into the functioning of the Board, which is a sin we all deplore.

---

[2] In veering toward centralization of power within the Reserve System, the CMC rightly avoided the recommendation sometimes put forward that the Board as well as the Open Market Committee should be abolished, and our monetary affairs placed in the hands of a single executive. This country has shown a wise aversion to "czars", and still likes the idea of some checks and balances.

The facts of the matter as I have observed them, however, are that the Chairman of the Board really serves largely at the will or pleasure of the President now. The Chairman of the Board is the chief point of contact between the Board and the President, the Secretary of the Treasury, the Council of Economic Advisers, and all the most important officers of the executive branch of the Government, and only to a slightly lesser degree with the Congress. If he is persona non grata at the White House, his ability to carry out the duties of his office is so gravely damaged as to make it impractical and unwise for him to continue as Chairman. The present wording of the law concerning the term of office of the Chairman seems to me merely to mask this fact of life. I do not mean, however, that the Chairman of the Board must become a subservient political appointee; he retains the right and the duty to represent the Board fairly and forcefully in expounding its views and methods, and preserves the individual right of resignation without disloyalty to the President, or party, if he decides that his service as Chairman is no longer compatible with the economic policies being followed by the Government.

A reduction in the number of members of the Board from seven to five, and in the terms of office from fourteen to ten years, with eligibility for reappointment, should make a modest contribution to improving the quality of the Board membership. And, as the report of the CMC says, it is a suggestion which retains stability of membership, protects independence in expressing views and advocating policies which may not be popular, and provides some safeguard against superannuation.

The recommendation that a means be sought to make clear that the Board, as a whole, is not to be enmeshed with routine administrative matters, to conserve its members' time, and to arrange for the more expeditious disposition of its caseload of business, has merit. The success of the suggestion is bound up, however, with questions of the qualifications for Board membership, the size of the Board, and the extent to which the individual members participate with the Chairman in working out coordination of monetary policy with the general economic policies of the Government. One reason for the implied "congestion of detailed business at the top" at the Board is the druglike attraction of such business when sitting in your office pondering the broad issues of monetary policy becomes tedious.

There is no question in my mind that the present occupational and geographical qualifications for Board members have outlived whatever sound purpose they ever had. They represent an embryonic phase of thinking concerning the role of a central banking system in this country. The general statement of qualifications suggested by the CMC is much more in tune with the responsibilities of the Federal Reserve System, present or proposed, and with the need to abandon ideas of finding effective national monetary policies in an atmosphere of representation of special interests. The companion recommendation of increased salaries for Board members has become a standard item in all considerations of the membership of the Board. The consistency with which this recommendation has been ignored by the executive and legislative branches of the Government suggests that there is a roadblock to its acceptance which does not have to do with the specific merits of the recommendation.

The suggestion of the CMC concerning the Federal Advisory Council appears to be an attempt to rescue from possible eventual extinction a body which was established in the early days of the Federal Reserve System as a sop to the bankers who had been ruled off the Board on the theory that you don't make game wardens out of poachers. Although the Board can seek advice from whatever individuals or groups it chooses under its general powers, there is some merit in retaining a statutory body, outside the Government and the Federal Reserve System, with which the Board must consult from time to time, and which has statutory authority to ask questions, seek information, and proffer advice. I do not think, however, that it is necessary or desirable to change the method of election of members of the Federal Advisory Council. What is necessary and desirable is to smash the tradition, growing out of the early history of the System, that the members of the Council elected by the boards of directors of the Federal Reserve Banks should be commercial bankers. Relieved of this anachronism, the boards of directors of the District banks are much better able to select representatives of their Districts than is a board at Washington, and the privilege is a desirable one in the relations between the Board and the Districts. Turning the present election process around, so as to make the Board the final appointing authority, seems to me to be a picayune obeisance to an obsession with what the CMC calls the influence of the "private base" of the System.

Now we begin to get down to the meat in the coconut. The recommendation that the law should formally constitute the twelve Federal Reserve Bank presidents as a conference, to meet at least four times a year with the Board, is an unnecessary and spurious attempt to seem to increase the stature of the presidents of the Federal Reserve Banks, who are to be deprived of their most important function by the next recommendation of the Commission. The conference of presidents of Federal Reserve Banks has been in existence for years; it meets regularly to discuss matters of credit policy and Federal Reserve administration; it consults with the Board as a necessary corollary of their joint responsibilities. The sanctions of tradition and long practice have given it a place and stature in the working of the Federal Reserve System, to which statutory recognition can neither add nor detract.

Having paid a left-hand compliment to the presidents of the Federal Reserve Banks in this recommendation, the CMC in its next recommendation relegates them to the role of branch managers by proposing that all the main powers of the System in the field of monetary policy should be lodged in the Board, with only advisory participation by the presidents of the Reserve Banks. It does this, first, on the ground that these powers—determining rediscount rates, deciding open market policy, and fixing reserve requirements—"should be complementary and governed by the same considerations, that is by the same people in the same forum". And, second, the CMC says that the exercise of these powers belongs exclusively in the hands of public officials: that is, the Board, and that there should be no ambiguity about where this responsibility lies.

The Commission is right, of course, in saying that these powers should be and are complementary, and it is right in saying that they should be exercised by public officials, but the fog of compromise evidently concealed from the Commission the logical suggestion, based on successful experience, that the place to lodge these complementary powers is in the Federal Open Market Committee (as it would be constituted on the present formula, if the size of the Board were reduced from seven to five members). The Federal Open Market Committee has become the heart of the Federal Reserve System; cut it out and you have a skeleton. It is a unique development in central banking which has evolved out of the experience of the System with the needs of a country of the size and character of the United States.[3] It is made up of men having statutory responsibilities, who serve on the Committee as individuals under law, and who are public officials and public servants in every real sense. Finally, the present constitution of the Federal Open Market Committee observes the cardinal principle of central banking that those who determine monetary policy should not only coordinate their actions with the general economic policies of the Government, but should also have a direct contact with the private money market—a contact which comes from living in the market, operating in the market, knowing the people in the market, and being able to feel the pulse of the market by hand from day to day, and not by random telephone calls or reviewing cold statistics.

Here, I think, is a tender point with some members of the joint committee and indeed of the whole Congress, and with some people in the Federal Reserve, but it cannot be avoided. The first and most direct point of contact between the policies of the monetary authorities and our national and international monetary systems is the New York money market. This is no device of greedy men and no accident of geography which can be changed by legislative fiat. It reflects the necessity, in a money economy such as ours, of having a marketplace where the final and balancing transactions of

---

[3] This argument should not be confused with the ideas prevalent in the early days of the Reserve System concerning regional differences in monetary policy. Monetary policy must be national, except in minor degree, but the whole is still the sum of its parts, and regional conditions are important in formulating national policy.

our national and international accounts can be carried out by a variety of delicately constructed financial institutions. And the operating arm of the Federal Reserve System in the principal money market of the nation, and of the world, is the Federal Reserve Bank of New York. The Banking Act of 1935 recognized that inescapable fact, and the need for a living link between monetary policy and the money market, by requiring that the president of the Federal Reserve Bank of New York must be a continuing member of the Federal Open Market Committee. All Federal Reserve Banks are equal, but the Federal Reserve Bank of New York is first among equals.

I can only surmise why the CMC decided that the Federal Open Market Committee should be dismantled. The statement that the "distinction between the Board and the Federal Open Market Committee has outlived its usefulness" raises questions, but answers none. From the language of other sections of the report, I would guess that those members of the CMC, who might have argued for the retention of the Federal Open Market Committee if they had known more about it, were lulled into acceptance of its abandonment as a "package deal" by those who were united in promoting the idea that private influence still permeates the Federal Reserve System, and must be eliminated if the System is to discharge its public functions properly and merit the complete confidence of the Government and the nation.

The report first constructs a neat word pattern to describe the structure of the Federal Reserve System, and it then states that a basic issue concerning the System is the "degree of independence of the Federal Reserve . . .from the banking community which it both serves and regulates".

It is my view that the word pattern—a System with a regulated private base, a mixed middle component, and a controlling public apex—is neat, but inaccurate. In all of its operations in the area of monetary policy I assert that the Federal Reserve System (Board and Reserve Banks) is a public institution, as it must be to discharge the public functions vested in it by the Congress. Clearly, the Board is a public body. It is equally clear to me that the Federal Open Market Committee, on which the presidents of the Federal Reserve Banks serve, as individuals, by statutory appointment, is a public body and not a "mixed middle component". The report of the CMC seems to rest its contrary view on the statement that the presidents of the Federal Reserve Banks are not Government appointees, but are elected by and have their compensation fixed by the boards of directors of their Banks, subject to the approval of the Federal Reserve Board. If the Commission had pursued this lead further, it would have known that approval by the Board of appointments and salaries of presidents of Reserve Banks is not a perfunctory power. The Board has demonstrated on numerous occasions that it is an active veto power, so that there is final public control. But this is more quibbling with words than meeting the real issue. The real answer is that you do not achieve honesty and integrity and unswerving devotion to the public interest by way of appointment procedures, but by charging competent men with an undivided responsibility for public service. That is the case with respect to the presidents of the Federal Reserve Banks as they serve by statutory appointment on the Federal Open Market Committee. They have no allegiance to private business in these matters, except as they try to contribute to the attainment of high level production and employment, sustainable economic growth, and a stable price level by monetary means.

The report of the CMC goes on to fill out its pattern of the "public-private category" within the Federal Reserve System with a brief discussion of the Federal Reserve Banks, but it quickly admits that "very tangibly as well as legally the Reserve Banks are public service institutions, and that their private 'ownership' is a highly attenuated right". In a rather odd "on the other hand" the report goes on to say, however, that the salaries of Reserve Bank presidents and their staff salary scales are set at going market rates rather than Government levels; the Reserve Bank presidents are not public servants in the usual sense. In my book this is no more than pandering to confused public ideas about conflict of interest. The salaries of Federal Reserve Bank officials and staffs are set at going market rates so that the Banks can attract the quality of administrators and personnel needed to assure the qualities and services necessary for constructive participation in determining monetary policy, and efficient operation, in the communities in which they live. I would say that it is fortunate and in the public interest that they are able to do this, so that numbers of capable, competent men can make a career of service in the Federal Reserve System, away from the hazards of political appointment, without the support of family or personal wealth, and without engaging in outside activities of any kind to supplement their regular compensation. There is no entering wedge for conflict of interest here.

The only specific suggestion which the Commission makes concerning the Federal Reserve Banks is that the present form of stock ownership of the banks should be retired, and that membership in the System be continued by a non-earning certificate of, say, $500, the same for each member bank. This seems to me to be knocking down an already "attenuated" strawman, insofar as it represents a belief or a suspicion that somehow private interests have a nefarious influence in, or derive special benefits from, the Federal Reserve System. As my previous remarks have indicated, however, I would be concerned if insistence upon the present form of stock ownership were to be interpreted as supporting such belief or suspicion. I would rather have the stock subscription changed to a certificate of membership than to have any cloud over the character of the Reserve Banks as public institutions.

There is one other point here that is worth mentioning, however. I have referred to the statement in the report of the CMC that a basic issue with respect to the Federal Reserve System is its degree of independence from the banking community which it both serves and regulates. This statement tends to confuse the monetary powers of the Federal Reserve System and its bank supervisory powers. In discharging its duties as a bank supervisor the Federal Reserve System may be a Government agency with an agency-clientele relationship with the business concerns it both serves and regulates, in the words of the Commission, but in the vastly more important realm of monetary policy the Federal Reserve has no agency-clientele relationship with any one but the American people as a whole. If the bank supervisory powers of the

Federal Reserve System are the reason for concern about the "ownership" of the stock of the Federal Reserve Banks by the member banks, consideration should be given to consolidating the regulatory functions of Federal banking authorities outside the Federal Reserve System, as suggested in a footnote by some members of the CMC. The "regulated private base" of the System (the commercial banking system), in the word pattern of the Commission, is not the base of the System as a monetary authority. It is the private monetary mechanism which serves as a channel through which the monetary actions of the System spread out through the whole community, pervasively but without unnecessary intrusion upon private transactions between citizen and citizen.

Now let me close by coming back to the question of the Federal Open Market Committee, which is by far the most important question to which the CMC addressed itself in the section of its report on the structure of the Federal Reserve System. I do not believe that many of the members of the Commission realized the full import of what they were doing when, actively or passively, they acquiesced in recommending that the Federal Open Market Committee be abolished. I have said it is the heart of the Federal Reserve System as it has evolved over the years, and it is. It is the forum where representatives of the constituent parts of the System—the Reserve Board and the Reserve Banks—meet as individuals and equals, bearing identical responsibilities under law to decide questions of high monetary policy. It is the group within the System which brings to the consideration of policy knowledge of what is going on in Government, in the money market, and in commerce, industry, and agriculture throughout the country.[4] Its members take back to the Government, to the money market, and to the country, an understanding of what has been decided which is an essential ingredient of effective monetary policy.

[4] This form of words does not exclude labor or the consumer or any other group within the body economic, although organized labor has ordinarily been suspicious of the Reserve System, and has generally refused to become better acquainted, even when invited to do so.

I have said that if you remove the presidents of the Federal Reserve Banks from continuous (in the case of New York) or periodic (in the case of the others) participation in this high function you will tear down the spirit and morale of the twelve Banks, and I believe it. The men who are the most capable and imaginative officers of Federal Reserve Banks, and who staff their outstanding economic research departments, are not primarily interested in counting coin and currency, in sorting checks, and in examining member banks. They and their successors won't be attracted to jobs in which these operating chores are their only direct and primary responsibility: jobs in which they are only called upon as consultants and advisers in matters of monetary policy. Participation in the work of the Federal Open Market Committee, with authority and responsibility—the right to vote as well as to talk—is what attracts the best men to the chief offices of the Federal Reserve Banks, and it is this contact which fills their official staffs with a sense of dedication and high purpose.

I sincerely hope that the Congress of the United States will never reverse itself on this important matter. I sincerely hope that it will go forward to complete the ingenious work of the Banking Act of 1935, by combining in law in the Federal Open Market Committee the complementary powers of the Federal Reserve System with respect to open market operations, rediscount rates, and reserve requirements.

Thank you for giving me this opportunity to present my views to your committee.

Yours faithfully,

Allan Sproul

Chapter 7

Foreign Aid

Allan Sproul was not by background an expert, at least no more than anyone else, in the field of foreign aid. Nevertheless, in early 1960 he visited India and Pakistan as a member of a three-man team appointed by the World Bank. With him were Herman Abs, Chairman of the Deutsche Bank of Frankfurt, and Sir Oliver Franks, Chairman of Lloyds Bank of London. Their mission was to examine the role of foreign aid in the economic development of India and Pakistan, and they came to be known as "The Three Wise Men".

This chapter contains a letter he wrote to Alfred Hayes from New Delhi in the middle of his trip, an address he delivered to the World Affairs Council shortly after he returned, and his testimony in the spring of 1963 before a committee appointed by President Kennedy to advise the Government on foreign aid.

On his trip to India he met with Prime Minister Jawaharlal Nehru, and his reactions are of historical interest as well as providing insight with respect to Sproul himself: "India has had the good fortune—one might say the providential good fortune—to have as its leader in all of the years since partition, Mr. Nehru. Many of us have blown hot and cold on Mr. Nehru as a result of what seemed to be his Hamlet-like indecision in matters involved in a world collision of totalitarianism and democracy, and because of what we had read of his economic views, which seemed to derive a great deal from Marxism. After meeting with him and after seeing something of his people and country, however, I am willing to accept the judgment that his intelligence and integrity have usually overcome political and economic dogma. His favorite label for his economic program now seems to be 'pragmatic' and, unlike some of his associates, I believe he has demonstrated his ability to change course when necessary in order to abandon untenable positions. So far as I am concerned, he has performed a political miracle in holding his country together and bringing it along the path of democratic accomplishment as far as it has now progressed."*

Sproul's overall views on the subject of foreign aid were summed up in a letter he wrote on July 6, 1965 to Murray J. Rossant, then of the *New York Times*: "Perhaps the two myths which need most to be dispelled, if we are to move toward a better public appreciation of the program, are that foreign aid is primarily a humanitarian exercise and that dollars will do the job in the absence of an adequate organization in this country to administer their allocation and in the absence of people in the recipient countries who can effectively and usefully manage their expenditure. A.I.D. [Agency for International Development] officials have long argued that they are spending about as much as can properly be spent, while the mushy fringe of the liberal community talks about the niggardliness of spending anything less than, say, 1 percent of our GNP. And the take-off advocates have sidestepped the fact that it is primarily people that have to take off in the less developed countries; that the shortages have been more human than financial. There is significance in the fact that the Peace Corps is the most imaginative and relatively the most effective thing we have done in this area."

* Excerpt from a talk by Sproul before the World Affairs Council, June 23, 1960. This excerpt is contained in a part of the talk which is not included as reprinted.

Letter to Alfred Hayes

Ashoka Hotel
New Delhi
March 15, 1960

Dear Al:

Thank you for your birthday letter! We had been out of touch on a jaunt around India and East Pakistan for two weeks, and mail from home was most welcome.

This has been an exciting, interesting, strenuous, tiring trip. Fourteen-hour days were not unusual, with frequent plane hops and overnight stops. I have stood up well, however, except for a two-day layover and lie-down in Karachi, where I contracted the "disease of the east".

Charlie Coombs has been a great help and a good traveling companion. He too had one brief bout with the above-mentioned ailment, but usually has managed to come through with nothing more than a tired feeling. Our colleagues have been pleasant and stimulating and so have our hosts. The countries we have visited are, as you know, countries of almost unbelievable contrasts.

We are spending this week in New Delhi, pulling ourselves and our ideas together and we hope to finish up at the weekend. After a stop in London, it looks as if I shall be getting to New York about the time you leave. I am sorry that this is so, but maybe I shall get in a day or two early and catch a few minutes with you.

Thank you for the press copy of the Annual Report. It is surprising how quickly one can forget the affairs of a country which have occupied most of his life, when he becomes immersed in the affairs of a country such as India. I had almost forgotten net borrowed reserves.

With best regards,

Sincerely,

Allan

Address delivered before the World Affairs Council, San Francisco, California June 23, 1960

India and Pakistan: Critical Testing Ground of Foreign Aid

I am not an expert on India and Pakistan, as anyone with any knowledge of these two countries, uneasy neighbors on the Indian subcontinent, could quickly find out. In fact, after visiting them, I have what I believe is a healthy skepticism of any outsider who thinks he is an expert on countries with such complicated backgrounds and diverse problems. They do not lend themselves to easy analysis and facile generalization.

Nor am I an authority on foreign economic aid to so-called underdeveloped countries. A considerable literature has grown up around this subject, and there has been a lot of sophisticated theorizing about it. But the factual information needed to support the theories is not available and won't be for a long time, if ever. The one clear fact is that theory has run quite a bit ahead of practice. Meanwhile, decisions with respect to foreign aid and development are being made largely on the basis of what appear to be the immediate political, military, and economic factors directly involved.

Well, if I am not an expert on India and Pakistan, and if I am not an authority on foreign economic aid, you might ask what I was doing on the Indian subcontinent last February and March, as a member of a three man bankers' mission, familiarly known as "The Three Wise Men", which attempted to gain some useful impressions concerning the economic progress of the two countries and the contributions of foreign economic aid to that progress. It is a somewhat involved story, but I shall try to tell it briefly as an illustration of policymaking in this field.

It all began in February 1959, when Senator John F. Kennedy, now aspiring to higher office, and Senator Cooper, a former United States Ambassador to India, introduced a resolution in the Senate, recommending that a mission composed of representatives of the United States and other friendly, democratic countries consult with the governments of South Asia on their economic problems. The Senate Committee on Foreign Relations considered the resolution and, in September 1959, it was passed by the Senate, as amended.* The resolution stated that it is the sense of the Congress that the President of the United States should explore with other friendly and democratic countries, and appropriate international organizations, the desirability and feasibility of establishing an international mission to consult with the governments of countries in the area of South Asia on their needs in connection with the fulfillment of currently planned and anticipated development programs, and to consider and recommend ways and means of jointly assisting in the implementation of these plans in cooperation with the governments of South Asia.

This was a pretty tall order. The area of South Asia was thought of as including India, Pakistan, Burma, Afghanistan, Nepal, and Ceylon. The friendly democratic nations, besides the United States, presumably included nations of the Common Market in Western Europe, nations of the British Commonwealth, and donor members of the Colombo Plan, including Japan. Meanwhile, India and Pakistan, the key members of the South Asia group, had gotten well into the development of their respective third and second Five Year Plans. The conception of a high-powered mission from aid-granting countries, which would be able to "make a deal" with aid-receiving countries in South Asia regarding the size and shape of their development programs and regarding the volume and character of Western aid, ran out of time and support.

A more modest idea then began to take shape. It confined the survey of economic problems and progress in South Asia to India and Pakistan; it narrowed down the members of the mission to nationals of three of the principal industrial and aid-granting countries—the United Kingdom, West Germany, and the United States—and the mission became a private mission which would neither represent nor be authorized to speak for governments.

* A similar resolution was introduced in the House of Representatives by Congressman Chester Bowles, another former United States Ambassador to India, but failed to reach a vote because of lack of time before adjournment of the session.

There was still some difficulty, however, as to who would take the initiative in appointing the members of the mission and arranging for their reception in India and Pakistan. The governments of these countries, I believe, indicated their willingness to receive such a mission and their unwillingness to request that it be sent. It was finally decided that the President of the International Bank for Reconstruction and Development, Mr. Eugene Black, should invite three bankers, one each from the United Kingdom, West Germany, and the United States, to visit India and Pakistan in February and March of this year. The three governments welcomed Mr. Black's initiative, and the governments of Pakistan and India indicated their willingness to receive the mission as guests of government and to give it every opportunity to learn about their economic development programs and their use of foreign aid. That is how Mr. Herman Abs, Chairman of the Deutsche Bank of Frankfurt, Sir Oliver Franks, Chairman of Lloyds Bank Limited of London, and I happened to go to the Indian subcontinent. As missions go, and they go often to such countries as India and Pakistan, we were unique. Since officially we represented nobody, in a sense we represented everybody.

In the letter which we wrote to Mr. Black at the conclusion of our visit on March 19, 1960, we phrased our assignment in this way:

> *The proposal that we should visit India and Pakistan was sponsored by you, as President of the International Bank for Reconstruction and Development, and was welcomed by the Governments of India and Pakistan. We accepted the invitation as independent and private individuals. We received no terms of reference or instructions either from the International Bank or from the Governments of our own countries. We have, therefore, had to consider what an independent mission of this kind, with a limited amount of time at its disposal, could most usefully attempt. You told us that we were not expected to submit a formal report: and, indeed, it would have been impossible for us in the*

course of a month to undertake any detailed assessment of the economic situation and development programs of India and Pakistan. We have concluded that the most useful task which we can set ourselves is to try and form broad general impressions about the problems of development in these two countries. In doing so, we have approached the question of the scale and balance-of-development plans in qualitative rather than quantitative terms, and we have tried to see how the kind of proposals for development which are at present under consideration in these two countries fit into the broad pattern of what has already been achieved. We hope that the bundle of impressions which we have formed will help toward the understanding of some of the problems of policy which seem to us to confront both the countries which we have visited and those countries and international institutions which are, or may be, concerned with providing finance for development.

What I have to say, now, will be based on the impressions of this mission, and its advisers, because we each had an adviser known variously as "the three wise guys" and the "wise men, second class" and known by us as our good right arms. I shall add to my report on these impressions one or two personal opinions based on my trip but not included in the letter which the mission wrote and signed without individual reservation or dissent.

And let me inject one such opinion right here. The cynical response to the observations of such a mission as ours is that the Indians and Pakistanis showed us only what they wanted us to see. Of course they showed us what they wanted us to see, and we wanted to see what they thought were favorable examples of their development and their use of foreign aid. You can't see everything in six weeks, even though your days are filled from early morning to late at night, seven days a week, as our days were. But you can't travel about for hundreds of miles in the cities and through the villages and farmlands of India and Pakistan without seeing the pitiful condition of multitudes of human beings, the poverty, dirt, and disease, and the primitive methods still in use in agriculture and some industries, which make hopes of progress seem almost doomed. These things had to be seen—not to be believed. We saw them.

Now, in order that you may have some basis for judging my personal views, as well as my report on some of the views of the mission, I should also tell you my general attitude with respect to foreign economic aid. So far as the countries we aid are concerned, I agree with those who say that the purposes of our aid, broadly, are to develop constructive forces that will further political and social stability in these countries, to support their military strength, and to enlarge the productive and technical bases of their economies so as to improve the standards of living of their people and thus to demonstrate that expectations of a better life can be realized without resort to totalitarian methods.

So far as we are concerned, I think that the primary justification for foreign economic aid is our national security which includes survival of our national values—that we have no moral obligation to raise the standard of living of other nations up to our own. I think that whatever economic advantages we derive from such aid, and I believe there will be such advantages in the long run, are supplementary. I think that, if foreign aid coincides with the humanitarian instincts of our people, that is fine and contributes to our strength as a nation, but it is not the purpose and province of government continuously to distribute the resources of this country for humanitarian purposes. Nor do most foreign peoples believe that governments do things for humanitarian purposes. As has well been said, "If we do not reveal a good, solid motive of self-interest, they are apt to invent one for us and this can be more sinister than anything we could even dream of ourselves." Finally, I do not belong to the school of roving economists and international philanthropists which believes that, if a billion dollars of foreign aid is good, two billion would be twice as good or maybe four times as good. Men are more important than money in a foreign-aid program and able and available men are even more scarce than money in both the aid-giving and the aid-receiving countries. You can go badly wrong giving too much money to men of too little capacity.

With that testament in the record I can get on with my task. Despite the many differences and contrasts between India and Pakistan, there are also important economic similarities and I am going to talk first of the two countries, together, in order to keep my remarks within the confines of your time and patience and in order to try to keep the thread of my exposition clear.

The basic economic problem of both countries is the shortage of capital resources in relation to investment needs. There is the familiar vicious circle of low income, low investment, and continuing low income, which can only be broken effectively and in time by an inflow of help, of capital, from abroad. And right there you may well ask why this vicious circle must be broken by foreigners, and relatively quickly—why Indians and Pakistanis must try to accomplish, in say thirty or forty years, what it took us a hundred or a hundred and fifty years to accomplish. To this I can only say that times and circumstances have changed. These people, recently come to independence after a long period of colonialism, with the strident claims of what can be accomplished quickly by totalitarian methods flooding across their borders from Russia and China, are putting democratic or nontotalitarian processes to the test of relatively swift accomplishment in terms of economic progress. They may be trying to go too far too fast, but it would take a curious kind of simplicity, in the face of a most complex political and economic problem, to rely completely on this judgment, and to condemn their efforts wholly because of it.

Perhaps equally as important as the shortage of capital in their economic dilemma is the sheer size of their economic problem. Not only are the real incomes of the people low but, with a population of 500 million in the two countries, the capital resources required to generate even modest increases in real income are very large. And the problem is made more intractable by the rate of population growth. The governments are confronted with the task of trying to provide the additional food and services required by increases in population in the order of 2 percent per annum, while at the same time struggling to bring about an increase in per capita income.

It is the size of the task, as well as the need for swift accomplishment, which has made it more of a government undertaking, involving a larger degree of economic planning than we might think desirable. But here it is fair to say, I think, that there is a definite purpose in Pakistan to have as much business as possible take place in the private sector; and in India there seems to be a growing realization that both the public and the private sectors of the economy have their proper contribution to make to economic progress, and that a doctrinaire socialist approach is not the way to the economic heavens. . . .

Most of us know something of the handicaps of the Indian nation in achieving economic progress. The religious taboos—it is a commonplace that at least one third and perhaps one half of the cattle in India are surplus in relation to the feed supply. The caste system which still survives. The persistent elements of feudalism. The linguistic nationalism or regionalism. The illiteracy. The disease. The pitiless climate which saps energy. The cultural emphasis on immaterial things. The live-and-let-live philosophy which can mean an unhealthy tolerance of inefficiency and corruption.

There are countervailing assets, however, if we are going to do double-entry bookkeeping. India has probably much the best administrative organization for political, economic, and social development of any nation in Asia outside the Russo-Chinese bloc, except Japan. It has geographic unity and agricultural diversity. It has a relatively homogeneous governing class, both in power and in opposition, giving it a workable parliamentary system. Its people will work hard and have a shrewd common sense in most matters not affected by religious scruples. It is technically the most advanced country in Asia next to Japan, and possibly China. In the long run, it should be able to become a major manufacturing country, supplying industrial goods and equipment to Asia and Africa, and even farther afield.

I cannot give you an unequivocal answer to this problem in relativity, in justifiable self-interest, and in chances of success, nor do I think, can anyone else. The margins of error are great. The likely existence of items of lesser urgency in any such development program as that of India suggests strongly the possibility of trimming down the need for foreign aid. The requirements of prudence, because of possible bad harvests or faulty industrial planning and the thin layer of managerial talent, suggests that there may be smaller aggregate development plans which would provide sustainable progress. Or it may be that, for bargaining purposes and encouraged by the advice of some of the more enthusiastic planners from this country, the Indians have projected a larger figure of foreign aid than they expect to realize in their Third Year Plan. When you have said and weighed all this however, you will still be faced with a value judgment.

Given the key position of India in the whole Asian-African complex, and recognizing the inevitable comparisons which will be made between the economic progress of a democratic India and a totalitarian China, my own judgment is that the course followed by the 400 million people of India will have direct and indirect repercussions on the security of the United States. That is why I have come to the opinion that the risks and hazards of investing heavily in Indian development are justified, and for equivalent reasons in Pakistan also.

We have been doing just that, and I do not know that the increased size of India's Third Five Year Plan and Pakistan's Second Five Year Plan would require an increase in the amount of foreign economic aid extended by the United States. The time has come when other industrial nations of the Free World can and should participate more heavily in this investment, and there are indications that this is being recognized and given effect. In this case I also welcome the assistance which the Russians and some of their satellites are giving to India. I do not think that such assistance will outweigh, in the aggregate, the aid given by the free nations, and I do not think it will sway the political development of India, one way or the other, but it will share the burden and the risk of India's need for foreign assistance. It is my guess, and it can be nothing more, that there will be no left turns in India if democratic processes and programs can, within some reasonable period of time, bring about a modest increase in the standard of living of the Indian people. Left turns have always been unpopular in Pakistan, of course.

There should be no mistaking, however, that our program of aid to India, and Pakistan too, is a project of long term as well as huge size. We have all heard a great deal about so-called "take-off points" in countries such as India and Pakistan; the theoretical concept that, if enough investment funds are poured into a country over a relatively short period of time, self-sustaining growth will develop and eliminate the need for further foreign aid. I have doubts about the practical application of this whole concept, and I am certain that we would be fooling ourselves if we approached the development problems of India—and of Pakistan—in terms of a Marshall Plan designed to reach certain targets of viability and self-sustaining growth within a fixed period of years. The simple fact that per capita income in both countries is so low will almost inevitably mean that development will be a slow laborious process probably extending many years into the future. As in other facets of the contest between communism and democracy, we should be girding ourselves for a protracted conflict, not expecting to win quickly like the "good guys" in a television western.

A necessary ingredient of a successful attack on these long-range problems, I think, is that as a nation and as individuals we should understand that it will require sacrifices to achieve our objectives. This year, 1960, would be a good year to try to achieve that understanding. We shall be choosing our national leaders and our national legislators for another election period. We should be demanding leaders and legislators who will dare to tell us that great achievement may demand great sacrifices. So far I have not detected the clear sound of this note in the campaign oratory and literature.

Instead there is a good deal of juggling with figures of national production and income, apparently intended to convince us that our rate of economic growth can be readily increased so that there will be plenty of available resources with which to do everything we might want to do at home and abroad, without anybody having to give up anything. Military needs and domestic civilian needs will be met handily out of the same ever-normal treasury. Foreign economic aid will be increased, while the current deficit in our balance of payments will wither away without check to our habits of conspicuous consumption. Such a prospectus is a fraud in the face of bitter and protracted conflict which lies ahead with those who talk peaceful coexistence while they seek to destroy us.

A provocative writer on these matters, Barbara Ward, has written that: "Western economies cannot make a fetish of a 3 percent rate of growth if real, demonstrable human needs call for a higher rate; and there seems little doubt such needs exist." The implications of such statements as this, for most of those seeking political office, seems to be that an increase in our rate of economic growth is what is needed and possible, in order that we may be spared the necessity of making hard choices in attacking our current economic problems.

This is not a matter of fetishes, however, but of what the National Bureau of Economic Research calls a respect for facts. We know something about our past rate of economic growth, and something about the present rate, and our knowledge does not encourage too sanguine hopes of an early and substantial increase. We do not know anything about our future rate of economic growth, although there is no lack of fancy as to what the potential rate could be. We may be able to do better than we have done in the past, and we hope we shall, but it won't be easy and it won't be quick.

Meanwhile, if we are going to continue to maintain our military security, increase the resources we devote to socially desirable objectives at home, provide foreign aid in the magnitudes which can be effectively administered, and preserve our international solvency and our domestic stability, we shall have to postpone some of our ideas of increased leisure, and curb some of our desire for an ever-increasing volume of consumer goods and services, in favor of our longer term goals.

From what I know, and have seen and heard, I would counsel making such sacrifices in order to do our share in aiding the economic development of India and Pakistan.

Aide-mémoire on foreign aid prepared as background for testimony before the Committee to Strengthen the Security of the Free World, headed by General Lucius Clay, and appointed by President Kennedy on December 10, 1962. A note transmitting the document to Alfred Hayes is dated April 19, 1963.

I realize that foreign aid policy is a "complex combination of military, political and economic measures which must be complementary and reinforcing", and that it cannot be treated fully in a brief memorandum.

I realize that the President recently appointed a new chief of the A.I.D., who seems to have excellent qualifications for the job, and that the A.I.D. has been working on a plan which would concentrate our aid in fewer places, with greater operating efficiency and more competent personnel.

I realize that your committee is composed of men with a special range of experience in these matters and special means of determining "whether the level and distribution of the foreign aid program is contributing to the security of the United States, and is directed to specific and attainable goals of economic and political stability in the Free World".

Nevertheless, it has seemed to me that the views of an individual who has a general knowledge of what has been done and what is now being done might be of help to you, particularly as you may be concerned with foreign economic aid insofar as it can be separated from military aid. At least I suffer from no restraints of appointment in expressing my opinions.

My questions about our foreign aid policies go well beyond the administration of the foreign aid program, susceptible as its administration has been to a variety of organizational and executive changes over the past fifteen years which might well have disrupted a more substantially based operation. It has seemed to me that our present policies have suffered from our first success, from a faulty emphasis on the virtues of economic development of backward countries as a shield against communism and a contribution to our military defenses, from the mixing of vague moral and humanitarian motives with the vital interests of the United States, and from our inability to explain clearly to the Congress and to the public exactly what we are doing, what we have done, and why.

Our first foreign aid success was the Marshall Plan, which contributed so much to the rebuilding of the war-shattered economies of Western Europe. That success offered no guide to subsequent programs, unless it was a misleading one. The economies of the nations we were then helping were a part of the social fabric of countries with stable political institutions, and their economic systems were manned by people with managerial talent and technical skills equivalent to our own. And, most important, their values and their aspirations were much the same as ours. But the public image of foreign aid has continued to be distorted by the success of the Marshall Plan; by the belief that, given certain efforts at social reform and self-help by the recipient countries, injections of capital (and technical assistance) from abroad will put backward countries on the road in a relatively short time (say the ten years of the Alliance for Progress) to a viable economic existence.

This false guide was supported by the political use of partially hedged theories concerning so-called take-off points in the economic development of nations. It is only recently that there has come to be some public criticism, by people who have been exposed to the practical problems of foreign aid, of those persuasively presented views. What was omitted in the popular version of the theory was that economic take-off depends, fundamentally, on peoples' values—what they want, and the means of getting what they want in accordance with their capacities, their traditions, their religious beliefs, and their moral codes, if any. Capital and technology are now being demoted to the bottom of the list of basic needs for economic development and growth, being preceded by general literacy, a reliable apparatus of government and public administration, a clear development of objectives toward which the mass of the people is willing to work, and pride in the attainments necessary to reach those objectives. Admittedly, the values of whole peoples are not easy to determine and, over time, they may be modified, but to attempt to impose our values on a variety of foreign cultures smacks of impertinence and is doomed to failure. (It rivals and draws sustenance from the missionary spirit which conceives of the Jewish-Christian ethic as the only revealed religion.)

Even if preoccupation with the capital needs of people in the underdeveloped countries is not an invitation to failure, the philosophical idea that foreign economic aid will yield desirable results in terms of freedom, stability, democracy, and peace has a shaky foundation. The dynamics of industrial development, and the movement of peoples from villages to cities which it entails, create tensions and ferment (somewhat as it did in Western Europe and the United Kingdom during the industrial revolution). The revolutionary progeny of these tensions and ferments may take on the wrong coloration. Leaders in new nations, or those who overthrow governing groups in older but underdeveloped nations, usually gain much of their popular support by opposing foreign influence and foreign domination, call it Yankee imperialism, or neo-colonialism, or whatever. If they haven't the ability or the means to make good the improvement in the lot of the people, which they have also promised in their revolutionary phase, and if anti-foreign attacks begin to lose their power, they usually try to hold on by force and by denying those freedoms and those forms of democracy which they formerly espoused. This sort of thing is likely to lead to endemic political and economic instability. Our existing programs have been exposed to and have not shown much ability to deal with this sequence of events.

The vague moral and humanitarian motives, which have confused past aid policies, have ranged from the presidential dictum in his inaugural address that rich nations should help poor nations "because it is right", to the advice of a host of official and unofficial advisers that one of the two most immediate problems of worldwide scope facing modern man is the disparity between the "have" and the "have not" nations, and that we "need the challenge of world development to improve the quality of our national life". (Ambassador Stevenson might have said this although I don't know that he did.) About these noble sentiments there can certainly be two points of view, depending somewhat on whether you believe that we must still rely on the nation state to bond masses of people under civil discipline, or whether you think the nation state is becoming obsolete, that we should be leading the way to the millenium of the world state, and that we can move in that direction by shuffling off some of the problems of foreign aid to world organizations. My own view is that we must still get along, largely, with the nation state.

The government of a nation state, in order to "do good" abroad, has to do most of it directly or in a consortium with other nation states, and has to find that what it proposes to do serves the interests of the state itself in terms of security or trade or something more specific than "improving the quality of the national life".

Meanwhile the advice of, say, a Barbara Ward that devoting 1 percent of the national product to foreign aid is little enough to do, or of, say, an Oliver Franks that the northern hemisphere should now do for the southern hemisphere what the eastern hemisphere (northern branch) did for the western hemisphere in the nineteenth century is of little use or relevance. The first generalization is like saying that if we spent less on chewing gum we could spend more on education and health—it dodges the question of how choice is to be exercised in a democracy. The second generalization avoids the fact that the success of the injection of European capital into the northern part of the western hemisphere was due to the virtual extermination of the native population and its replacement by Europeans. In the southern part of the western hemisphere, where the native population was assimilated, or vice versa, the problem of underdevelopment is still with us after four centuries and the outlook for democracy and stability is still uncertain.

Nor can clothing this sort of vague aspiration in the cloak of "enlightened self-interest" get us out of our difficulties of precision in defining objectives, devising means of attaining them, and establishing criteria for cutting off aid when attainment becomes unlikely. Taking the simplest argument in support of self-interest, it is said that in building up the economies of the underdeveloped countries we are creating wider world markets and thus widening of the range of our own economic development. This can only be true if increases in population do not equal or outrun increases in production in the backward areas. There is no present evidence that this will be the case in many of them. Birth control "involves the whole adult population of a country and demands forethought and directed will power". It is "unlikely to be carried out successfully in the countries that need it most urgently".

I realize that this catalogue of faults of our foreign aid program is largely based on subjective reasoning, and I realize that we could not (and I would not) abandon our foreign aid efforts. I do think, however, that it is past time for us to subject the program to a more vigorous examination as to its fundamental premises than it has had thus far, so that we can begin modifying it in substance in the light of the findings of such an examination. This is what I hope your committee has in mind.

My own suggestions are:

(1) That we recognize that we are not going materially to better the lot of millions of people in the underdeveloped countries over the next few decades—it is a long-term process at best.

(2) That the important question for us is not whether the Congress appropriates $4.9 billion or some lesser figure for foreign aid in a given year, but whether we can put together a program which has sufficiently clear and definite objectives and sufficient chances of a moderate success, so that it will command the vigorous support of the public and the Congress. Here I realize that the power of the central government has come to depend, to a considerable extent, on appeals to the people by the President couched in lofty terms and consisting of unsupported generalizations, but it seems clear that the effectiveness of this approach is wearing out in the case of foreign aid appropriations (or your committee would probably not exist).

(3) That such a program, geared to a time factor of the rest of the century, say, instead of a decade, and taking more account of the values of the peoples of dif-

ferent countries and less of theories of economic take-off based on our own values, will shift the emphasis from aid dollars of which we have a lot, to competent people in this country and in the recipient countries, of which there are not too many. An A.I.D. organization, conceived in these terms, should be developed on a career basis. We would give up the idea of trying to do it in a relatively few years with temporary or borrowed personnel. And, in my opinion, it should be an organization with autonomy, directly under the President, and coordinating its affairs with the State Department and Defense and Treasury as they now coordinate with one another.

(4) That it is neither possible nor desirable to develop and service such a program effectively when it covers upward of 100 countries. This is an invitation to random decisions on a shotgun basis aiming at a vague general target. And it is likely to result in a lot of foreign governments being encouraged to undertake tasks beyond their capabilities, which leads to waste through incompetence and to an extension and tightening of government authority over the individual. What is needed, I would say, is a clearer definition of objectives, a clearer understanding of the means and the chances of attaining them, and a culling out of the countries which are receiving aid. The priorities should be determined on the basis of selecting countries where the stakes are high, where the scale of our real interests is great, and where the chances of aid being used effectively are moderately good (India for example). In the case of these countries, we should aid them with whatever it takes, within their capacity to absorb aid, and not niggle about the degree of their alignment with us. (I find it hard to justify the amounts of economic aid we have been extending to Korea, Formosa, Vietnam, Laos, Turkey, and Spain, quite apart from military aid, and I think in some cases it may have been a disservice to them.)

(5) If anything could be done, at this late date, to pull the President back from his hasty alliance with the

Alliance for Progress, it would be a blessing. It has such a slim chance of success overall in the ten years allotted that it is becoming a weight in the whole foreign aid program and a symbol of failure. Yet, we do not seem to have any intermediate objectives to insert in place of those which have begun to demonstrate a lack of validity.

(6) If it appears, on examination, that our failures have been failures of a concept of foreign aid based on faulty generalizations and inapplicable expressions of high moral purpose, that we do not blame such failures on not having done enough, or not having done it effectively, or not having been firm enough in dealing with recipients, or not having the right sort of organization. That is the way a program which contains some good and had some hope has become a near casualty.

As it stands, our foreign aid program is reminiscent of Great Britain's first embassy to China by Lord Macartney in 1793-94. The British government wanted to remove the restrictions to which trade with China was subject and to establish a permanent embassy in Peking. The mission accomplished neither of these ends. Lord Macartney was taken to be an envoy bearing tribute and was sent home with a message from Emperor Chiien Lung to George III:

"We have never valued ingenious articles, nor do we have the slightest need of your country's manufactures. . . .You, O King, should simply act in conformity with our wishes by strengthening your loyalty and swearing perpetual obedience so as to ensure that your country may share the blessings of peace."

Chapter 8

International
Financial
Problems

From his earliest days at the Federal Reserve Bank of New York, where his first assignment was in the foreign department, Allan Sproul was intrigued by the intricacies of international finance. By all accounts he was more interested in the international implications and ramifications of monetary policy, especially the interrelations between domestic and international policies, than in any other aspect of central banking.

In light of that interest, frequently expressed in private, it might be considered surprising that he did not write more about international matters for public consumption during his years as head of the New York Bank. However, during that period—with the war, the peg, the Accord, and then the "bills only" controversy—serious thinking about international financial problems necessarily had to give way to more immediate concerns. If he had remained at the Bank beyond 1956, it is likely he would have had more to say publicly on the subject. As it was, it became a major topic in his personal correspondence and in his talks to the Wells Fargo Board of Directors.

The first of his papers reprinted in this chapter is an address he delivered to the annual convention of the American Bankers Association in 1949, entitled "Gold, Monetary Management, and the Banking System". It attracted wide attention at the time, mostly favorable, but also provoked a pamphlet entitled "Sproul Ignores Common Honesty" that he enjoyed making reference to for years thereafter.

The 1949 address to the American Bankers Association is followed by three talks delivered to the Board of Directors of the Wells Fargo Bank, one in 1975 and two in 1977. The last of these, in mid-November 1977, was delivered only months before he died, on April 9, 1978, at the age of eighty-two.

In that talk he sounded a note that he had expressed on a number of occasions: "Summit meetings and meetings of finance ministers from Rangoon to Rambouillet, and pronouncements of the IMF, have exhorted the nations to coordinate their domestic economic policies with their international economic responsibilities. The overall result has been a surplus of communiqués and not much concrete action. Now, in its own defense, the United States should take the lead in seeking a contribution to the solution of this general problem. It will have to bring about a major improvement in its own international position, and in the strength of the dollar which is still the center of the world's monetary machinery. It will have to quit dragging its feet and get on with the business of adopting an effective energy policy. . . .we shall have to move quickly and decisively to adopt an energy policy which will begin the process of curtailing the enormous volume and value of our oil and gas imports. There are grave domestic questions involved in existing energy proposals. But so far as the balance of payments is concerned the evidence is unambiguous and clear. The bargains and compromises must be struck. Time is running out."

Address to the Seventy-fifth Annual
Convention of the American Bankers Association
San Francisco, California, November 2, 1949

Gold, Monetary Management, and
the Banking System

As a native Californian—and a native San Franciscan—I have tried to think of something I might discuss which would be of special interest to our generous hosts at this convention. The fact that this is 1949, and that the whole State of California has been engaged in a two-year round of celebrations of the 100th anniversary of the discovery of gold in California, and of its immediate consequences, gave me an obvious lead. Gold is something in which we are all interested. Nor is this an untimely topic on other grounds. The recent wave of currency devaluations which swept around the world, following upon the devaluation of the British pound sterling six weeks ago, has fanned into modest flame the always smouldering fires of the gold controversy. In addition, I was eager to review the gold question because it is a good starting point for an understanding of the place of the Federal Reserve System in the monetary and economic life of the country.

As central bankers, of course, charged with responsibility for our monetary and credit policies, we have the question of gold under more or less constant surveillance. Most of the time, in recent years, we have been under attack from two sides because of our attitude toward gold. Those interested primarily or initially in the price of gold, and in what they call a free gold market, have fired from one side. Those interested primarily and eternally in gold coin convertibility—in a full and automatic gold standard domestically and internationally—have fired from the other. More recently, we have had a brief respite from attack while these two groups fired at each other, each group arrogating to itself responsibility for the only true gospel according to St. Midas. What I have to say will probably bring that brief respite to an end. The fire will again be concentrated on the monetary authorities, for whom I cannot presume to speak except as one individual engaged in the practice of central banking, but who will, no doubt, be blamed for my views.

Let me take account of each of these two groups separately; those who concentrate, at least initially, on a free gold market, and those who will have none of this heresy, but who want a fixed and immutable gold price and convertibility of currency—and therefore of bank deposits—into gold coin.

The first group, which includes the gold miners, makes its argument on several grounds, trying to combine economics and psychology with self-interest. Let me paraphrase their principal arguments as presented at hearings on bills to permit free trading in gold in the United States and its territories. In this way I may avoid the fact as well as the appearance of building straw opponents. The arguments most frequently presented in favor of these bills were:

(1) In the face of rising production costs and fixed selling prices, the gold mining industry has been forced to curtail its operations, and to the extent that it has operated, its profits have been reduced. The higher gold prices which would presumably prevail in a free market would correct this situation. This is the "do something for the gold miners" argument at its baldest.

When this argument is embroidered a little, it is claimed that, since the prices of all goods and services have increased so substantially during the past ten or fifteen years, it is necessary to open the way for an increase in the price of gold so as to be sure there will be enough gold to carry on the country's business; to bring the price of gold into adjustment with the prices of everything else.

(2) A second group of arguments expresses concern over the unsettling effects of the "premium" prices which are paid for gold abroad, and claims that a free gold market in the United States, with no gold export restrictions, would cause these premium markets abroad to disappear, with beneficial effects upon world trade and international relations.

(3) Third, there is an argument in equity—that gold miners should be allowed to sell their product at the best price they can obtain, as do producers of other products; and that American citizens, like the citizens of most other countries, should be free to hold or to buy and sell gold.

(4) Finally, there were those who viewed and favored a free gold market as a first step in the direction of a full gold coin standard, and who held that even a free market would act as a "fever chart" of the economy and lead to reform of extravagant Government fiscal policies, remove inflationary tendencies fostered by a managed currency, and lead to sounder conditions, generally.

To take these arguments up in order, it should be pointed out right away that it is quite possible that a free market for gold in the United States would not result in a rise in the price of gold, if for no other reason than that the Secretary of the Treasury is required, by law, to maintain all forms of United States money at parity with the gold dollar which contains $\frac{1}{35}$ of an ounce of fine gold. This means that the Treasury should maintain the price of gold at $35 a fine ounce in legal gold markets in the United States. To do this, if there were a legal free market for fine gold, the Treasury should sell gold to the extent necessary to maintain the market price at $35 a fine ounce. We might, therefore, get what would be in effect gold convertibility by way of a free market, but not a rise in the price of gold. Aside from this possible outcome of the establishment of a free market for gold, what is it we are being asked to do? In effect we are being asked to do something to benefit the gold mining industry, to encourage a shift of productive resources, in this and other countries, into gold production, in order to provide gold for hoarding. This, I submit, would be a witless proceeding, in terms of the welfare of the whole economy, matched only by our bonanza provisions for the special benefit of the miners of silver.

As for the economic embroidery of this request for aid to the gold mining industry, there is no lack of monetary means of carrying on the business of the country, nor is there likely to be. It is the economics of perpetual inflation to argue that a rise in the commodity price level should be followed by an arbitrary increase in the price of gold and hence in the reserve base, thus permitting and perhaps promoting additional deposit expansion and a further upward movement of prices. Even on the basis of statistics, which are not always reliable or comparable, it is interesting to note that the increase in the price of gold in the United States, in 1934, raised the price of gold by 69 percent, whereas wholesale prices in the United States are now only 60 percent above the 1927-29 level. We have been plagued, if anything, with an oversupply of money in recent years, and the United States gold stock, at the present price, is large enough to support whatever further growth of the money supply may be needed for years ahead.

The second group of arguments has to do with the desirability of knocking out of business the premium markets in gold which have existed and still exist in various foreign countries. I share the general dislike of these markets because they are parasites on the world's monetary system and help to siphon into gold hoards the resources of people who need food and clothing and equipment—and who wouldn't need so much help from us if they didn't use scarce foreign exchange to buy gold for private hoards. But I don't think the soundness nor the stability of the United States dollar is actually brought into question by these premium markets. At our official purchase price for gold—$35 a fine ounce—the United States has been offered and has acquired more gold than the total world production (excepting the U.S.S.R. for which reliable data on gold production, as on everything else, are not available), since 1934, the year of our devaluation. During those years—1934 to 1948 inclusive—estimated world gold production, valued at United States prices, was about $13.5 billion and United States gold stocks increased $16 billion. Most of the producers and holders of gold have been quite willing to sell us gold for $35 a fine ounce despite the quotations of $45 and $55 and so on up in the premium markets. The fact is that these premium markets represent insignificant speculative adventures around the fringe of the world supply and demand for gold. They reflect mainly the urgent and often illegal demands of a small group of hoarders, together with some private demand for gold to be used in relatively backward areas, or areas where the forms of civilized government have broken down, and where the metal serves the needs of exchange—or hoarding—better than a paper note. I do not think there would be any appreciable stimulus to United States gold production, if we opened the doors of this largely clandestine trade to our domestic gold miners. But, by legalizing it, we might well create what we are trying to destroy—uncertainty about the stability of the dollar and our own intentions with respect to its gold content.

The third argument—that the miners of gold should be free to sell their product at the best price they can get—is probably the giveaway. It is the argument that gold should be treated as a commodity when you think you can get a higher price for it, and as a monetary metal and an international medium of exchange when you want a floor placed under its price. I would say that you can't have it both ways. If you want the protection of an assured market at a fixed price, because gold is the monetary metal of the country, you should not ask permission to endanger the stability of the monetary standard by selling gold at fluctuating prices (the gold producers hope higher prices) in a fringe free market. Under present conditions, the only real price for gold is the price the United States Treasury is prepared to pay for it. So long as that is the case, there is no sense in a "make believe" free gold market, in which possible temporary or short-run deviations from the fixed price of the Treasury might have disturbing consequences.

Nor is the argument that citizens of the United States should have the same privileges as the citizens of other countries, when it comes to holding or trading in gold, at all convincing to me. It is true that in a number of foreign countries the holding of gold by private citizens is legal, and in some foreign countries strictly internal free trading in gold is permitted. In many cases, however, this merely represents the shifting around of a certain amount of gold which is already being hoarded in the country, since in practically all these countries the export and import of gold on private account is either prohibited or subject to license. And, in many countries where gold is produced, some percentage, if not all, of the newly mined gold must be sold to the monetary authorities, a requirement which further limits the amounts available for trading and hoarding. These restricted and circumscribed privileges in other countries are no reflection of a loss of inalienable rights by our people. They are attempts by these foreign countries to adjust their rules with respect to gold to their own self-interest and, so far as possible, to the habits of their people, all under the sheltering umbrella of a world gold market and a world gold price maintained by the Treasury of the United States. We have deemed it wise to maintain such a fixed point of reference in a disordered world. We have decided by democratic processes and by Congressional action that this policy requires, among other things, that gold should not be available for private use in this country, other than for legitimate industrial, professional, or artistic purposes. We have decided that the place for gold is in the monetary reserves of the country, as a backing for our money supply (currency and demand deposits of banks), and as a means of adjusting international balances, not in the pockets or the hoards of the people. If we want to reverse that decision, the means of reversal are at hand, but it should be a clear-cut and clean-cut reversal, restoring convertibility. Providing a dependent free gold market, in which gold miners and a little gold group of speculative traders or frightened gold hoarders (such as those who now take advantage of a provision in the regulations to buy and sell "gold in the natural state") could carry on their business is not the way to meet the problem.

I do not propose to get in the cross fire of those who claim that a free gold market would be a step toward convertibility and those who claim that a free gold market, without free coinage at a fixed price, would cause us to lose whatever modicum of a gold standard we now have and lead to monetary chaos. That is one of those doctrinal arguments in which the subject abounds. I will merely say here that I think authorization of a free gold market in this country, with no change in the present responsibility of the Secretary of the Treasury to maintain all forms of money coined or issued by the United States at parity with the "gold dollar", would probably lead indirectly to convertibility. The desirability of doing this is another matter, which I shall now try to discuss briefly and dispassionately. This is a hazardous attempt because there is no subject in the field of money and banking which so arouses the passions, and which so readily defies brief analysis.

Two groups of arguments for the reestablishment of a gold coin standard may, perhaps, be distinguished in the writings and speeches of those who propose it, one group relating primarily to the domestic economy and one to the probable effects on international trade and finance. In the first group the arguments run about as follows:

(1) Replacement of our "dishonest", inconvertible currency with an "honest" money having intrinsic value would promote confidence in the currency and encourage savings, investment, long-time commitments, and production.

(2) Irredeemable paper money leads to inflation, whereas the upper limits imposed upon currency and credit expansion by a thoroughgoing gold standard serve as a restraining influence on irresponsible politicians and overoptimistic businessmen.

(3) Present Governmental taxing and spending policies are wrong, and dangerous. The gold standard would put a brake on public spending.

(4) As a corollary of the preceding argument, since the gold standard would hinder further extension of Government control and planning, it is a necessary implement of human liberty.

The second group of arguments, relating to the international advantages of a gold coin standard, generally makes no distinction between the effects of a unilateral adoption of such a standard by the United States, and the multilateral establishment of an unrestricted gold standard by many countries, and of exchange rates fixed by such a standard. The arguments run somewhat as follows:

(1) The existence of premium markets in gold abroad and the lack of gold convertibility at home creates—and is representative of—lack of confidence in the gold value of the dollar. In the absence of a thoroughgoing gold coin standard, we cannot convince anyone that we may not devalue the dollar.

(2) Restoration of "normal" patterns of international trade is being retarded by the inconvertibility of currencies in terms of gold and, therefore, one with another. This inconvertibility has led to tariffs, quotas, exchange controls, and to general bilateralism.

(3) Under a managed paper currency system there is always the temptation to solve national problems by devices which lead to international disequilibrium. This, in turn, has led to domestic devices restrictive of foreign trade. The international gold standard, by eliminating the need for restrictive commercial policy, would increase the physical volume of international trade, resulting in an improved division of labor and higher standards of living for everyone.

First, let me say that I perceive no moral problem involved in this question of gold convertibility. Money is a convenience devised by man to facilitate his economic life. It is a standard of value and a medium of exchange. Almost anything will serve as money so long as it is generally acceptable. Many things have served as money over the centuries, gold perhaps longest of all because of its relative scarcity and its intrinsic beauty. In this country we still retain some attachment to gold domestically, and more internationally, but to carry on our internal business we use a paper money (and bank deposit accounts) which has the supreme attribute of general acceptability. There is no widespread fear of the soundness of the dollar in this country, no widespread flight from money into things. The constant cry of wolf by a few has aroused no great public response. Savings, investment, long-term commitments, and the production and exchange of goods have gone forward at record levels.

Much of the nostalgia for gold convertibility is based, I believe, on fragrant memories of a state of affairs which was a special historical case, a state of affairs which no longer exists. The great period of gold convertibility in the world was from 1819 to 1914. It drew its support from the position which Great Britain occupied, during most of the nineteenth century and the early part of the twentieth century, in the field of international production, trade, and finance. The gold coin standard flourished because the organization of world trade under British leadership provided the conditions in which it could, with a few notable aberrations, work reasonably well.

The ability of the British to sustain, to provide a focal point for, this system has been declining for many years, however, and the decline was hastened by two world wars which sapped the resources of the British people. The heir apparent of Great Britain, of course, was the United States, but up to now we have not been able to assume the throne and play the role. And until some way has been found to eliminate the lack of balance between our economy and that of the rest of the world, other than by gifts and grants-in-aid, we won't be able to do so. This is a problem of unraveling and correcting the influences in international trade and finance, which have compelled worldwide suspension of gold convertibility, not vice versa. The job before us now is to attack the problems of trade and finance directly. We should not deceive ourselves by thinking that gold convertibility, in some indefinable but inexorable way, could solve these underlying problems for us.

Nor is it true, of course, that gold convertibility prevented wide swings in the purchasing power of the dollar, even when we had convertibility. Within my own experience and yours, while we still had a gold coin standard, we had tremendous movements in commodity prices, up and down, which were the other side of changes in the purchasing power of the dollar. What happened to us in 1920-21 and 1931-33 under a gold coin standard should prevent a too easy acceptance of that standard as the answer to the problem of a money with stable purchasing power.

When you boil it all down, however, and try to eliminate mythology from the discussion, the principal argument for restoring the circulation of gold coin in this country seems to be distrust of the money managers and of the fiscal policies of Government. The impelling desire is for something automatic and impersonal which will curb Government spending and throw the money managers out of the temple, as were the money changers before them. To overcome the inherent weakness of human beings confronted with the necessity of making hard decisions, the gold coin standard is offered as an impersonal and automatic solution. Through this mechanism the public is to regain control over Government spending and bank credit expansion. It is claimed that whenever the public sensed dangerous developments, the reaction of many individuals would be to demand gold in exchange for their currency or their bank deposits. With the monetary reserve being depleted in this way, the Government would be restrained from deficit financing through drawing upon new bank credit; banks would become reluctant to expand credit to their customers because of the drain on their reserves; and the Federal Reserve System would be given a signal to exert a restraining influence upon the money supply. In this way, the Congress, the Treasury, and the Federal Reserve System would be forced by indirection to accept policies which they would not otherwise adopt.

In effect, under a gold coin standard, therefore, the initiative for overall monetary control would, through the device of free public withdrawal of gold from the monetary reserve, be lodged in the instinctive or speculative reactions of the people. No doubt some people would take advantage of their ability to get gold. There would be many reasons for their doing so. Conscientious resistance to large Government spending, or fear of inflation, might well be among these reasons. But speculative motives, a desire for hoards (however motivated), and such panic reactions as are generated by unsettled international conditions or temporary fright concerning the business outlook or one's individual security—all of these, and more—would be among the reasons for gold withdrawals. The gold coin mechanism does not distinguish among motives. Whenever, for any reason, there was a demand for gold, the reserve base of the monetary system would be reduced. Moreover, if only the United States dollar were convertible into gold while practically all other currencies were not, hoarding demands from all over the world would tend to converge upon this country's monetary reserves. Circumvention of the exchange controls of other countries would be stimulated, and dollar supplies which those countries badly need for essential supplies or for development purposes would be diverted to the selfish interests of hoarders.

Even if a particular reduction of the reserve base did occur for useful "disciplinary" reasons, the impact of such gold withdrawals upon the credit mechanism is likely to be crude and harsh. Since the present ratio between gold reserves and the money supply is about one to five, and since some such ratio will be in effect so long as this country retains a fractional reserve banking system, a withdrawal of gold coins (once any free gold is exhausted) will tend to be multiplied many times in its contractive effect on bank credit and the money supply. In a business recession, the Reserve System might undertake to offset this effect as it does now in the case of gold exports but, if the gold withdrawals attained sufficient volume, the shrinking reserve position of the Federal Reserve Banks would eventually prevent them from coming to the rescue.

It was, in part, to offset such arbitrary and extreme influences upon the volume of credit, and to make up for the inflexibility of a money supply based on gold coins (in responding to the fluctuating seasonal, regional, and growth requirements of the economy), that the Federal Reserve System was initially established. During the first two decades of its existence, the System devoted much of its attention to offsetting the capricious or exaggerated effects of the gold movements associated with continuance of a gold coin standard. We had an embarrassing practical experience with gold coin convertibility as recently as 1933, when lines of people finally stormed the Federal Reserve Banks seeking gold, and our whole banking mechanism came to a dead stop. The gold coin standard was abandoned, an international gold bullion standard adopted, because repeated experience has shown that internal convertibility of the currency, at best, was no longer exerting a stabilizing influence on the economy and, at worst, was perverse in its effects. Discipline is necessary in these matters but it should be the discipline of competent and responsible men; not the automatic discipline of a harsh and perverse mechanism. If you are not willing to trust men with the management of money, history has proved that you will not get protection from a mechanical control. Ignorant, weak, or irresponsible men will pervert that which is already perverse.

Here, I would emphasize my view that the integrity of our money does not depend on domestic gold convertibility. It depends upon the great productive power of the American economy and the competence with which we manage our fiscal and monetary affairs. I suggest that anyone who is worried about the dollar concentrate on the correction of those tendencies in our economic and political life which have brought us a deficit of several billion dollars in our Federal budget. at a time when taxes are high and production, employment, and income are near record levels. I suggest that, going beyond the immediate situation, they address themselves to the difficult problem of the size of the budget, whether in deficit or surplus or balance. At some point the mere size of the budget, in relation to national product, can destroy incentives throughout the whole community, a dilemma which is even now forcing curtailment of Government expenditures by the Labor government in Great Britain. These are problems gold coin convertibility cannot solve under present economic and social conditions. Gold has a useful purpose to serve, chiefly as a medium for balancing international accounts among nations and as a guide to necessary disciplines in international trade and finance. It has no useful purpose to serve in the pockets or hoards of the people. To expose our gold reserves to the drains of speculative and hoarding demands at home and abroad strikes me as both unwise and improvident.

Perhaps before I let go of this subject, which has held me and you overlong, I should say a word about merely raising the price of gold, without doing anything about a free gold market or gold coin convertibility of the currency. This is something which has intrigued Europeans and others who are "short of dollars", has interested some of our own people, and has become a South African war cry. An increase in the price the United States pays for gold would have two major results. It would provide the gold producing countries (and domestic producers), and the countries which have sizable gold reserves or private hoards, with additional windfall dollars with which to purchase American goods. And it would provide the basis for a manifold expansion of credit in this country which might be highly inflationary.

We have been engaged in an unprecedented program of foreign aid for the past four years. The Congress has authorized this aid at such times and in such amounts as were deemed to be in the interest of the United States. This is much to be preferred, I suggest, to the haphazard aid which would be granted by an increase in the price of gold, which must be on the basis of a more or less accidental distribution of existing gold stocks and gold producing capacity. If we raised the price of gold, every country which holds gold would automatically receive an increase in the number of dollars available to it. The largest increases would go to the largest holders which are the Soviet Union, Switzerland, and the United Kingdom. Every country which produces gold would automatically receive an annual increase in its dollar supply, and its gold mining industry would be stimulated to greater productive effort. The largest increases would go to the largest producers which are South Africa, Canada, and probably the Soviet Union. That would be an indiscriminate way to extend our aid to foreign countries, both as to direction and as to timing.

The domestic results of an increase in the price of gold would be no less haphazard. This country, as I have said, is not now suffering from a shortage of money and it has large gold reserves, which could form the basis of an additional money supply if we needed it. An increase in the dollar price of gold would increase the dollar value of our existing gold reserves in direct proportion to the change in price. There would be an immediate "profit" to the Treasury. The "profit" could be spent by Congressional direction or Treasury discretion. This would provide the basis for a multiple expansion of bank credit which, unless offset by appropriate Federal Reserve action, would expose our economy to the threat of an excessive expansion of the domestic money supply. The arbitrary creation of more dollars in this way would certainly be inappropriate under inflationary conditions, and would be an ineffective method of combating a deflationary situation.

At the moment, also, we should have in mind that there has just been an almost worldwide devaluation of currencies. Using the fixed dollar as a fulcrum, individual foreign countries have taken action designed to improve their competitive position *vis-à-vis* the United States, and to maintain their competitive position *vis-à-vis* one another. An increase in the dollar price of gold, which is devaluation of the dollar by another name, would undo the possible benefits of a venture in improved currency relationships which already has its doubtful aspects.

For all of these reasons it is encouraging to know that the Secretary of the Treasury has recently reiterated that the gold policy of the United States is directed primarily toward maintaining a stable relationship between gold and the dollar, and that for all practical purposes only the Congress can change that relationship. We have maintained an international gold bullion standard by buying and selling gold freely at a fixed price of $35 a fine ounce in transactions with foreign governments and central banks for all legitimate monetary purposes. This has been one fixed point in a world of shifting gold and currency relationships. We should keep it that way as another contribution to international recovery and domestic stability.

Remarks of Allan Sproul at the Board of Directors Meeting, Wells Fargo Bank, San Francisco, California, August 19, 1975

Having exhausted, at least temporarily and at least so far as I am concerned, the possible variations in treatment of a domestic economic situation which is struggling out of the rough and on to the fairway, I have assumed the task of bringing together some of the threads which make up the present pattern of the international monetary situation.

The international monetary system given form by the Bretton Woods Agreements of 1945, and based on convertible currencies at fixed parities and on the pediment of a reserve currency, the United States dollar, which was also the principal transactions currency of the world, served remarkably well for about a quarter of a century in terms of meeting the needs of expanding world trade and commerce.

But developments among the nations in a growing multinational and interdependent world probed the weak spots of the system, so that instead of building up stability over the years it moved toward instability and finally lost credibility. The necessary appearance of simple, effective performance, which causes people to think they know how the system works and to have faith in its workings, was lost in a series of financial crises which had to be patched up with *ad hoc* measures.

The final breakdown of the system was precipitated in August 1971, when the United States announced that it was no longer willing to buy and sell gold, freely, from and to foreign monetary authorities, the linchpin of the system. Subsequent attempts to prop up the Bretton Woods arrangements failed and, by early 1973, most of the countries of the world had abandoned fixed rates, the United States dollar had been devalued for the second time in fourteen months, and the world was awash on a sea of "managed" floating currencies.

Meanwhile, in view of the obvious deterioration of the old arrangements, the International Monetary Fund, or IMF, in September 1972 had set up a Committee on the

Reform of the International Monetary System, the so-called Committee of Twenty. It represented all of the 126 constituent member states of the IMF at the technical level. Its assignment was to consolidate earlier work on the problems which had developed and to design, as had been done at Bretton Woods, a new structure of international monetary cooperation, a task which was expected to take about two years to complete.

But the situation had so changed since Bretton Woods, and was continuing to change, and the war-engendered spirit of international cooperation of 1945 was so diluted, that the Committee had to admit in June 1974 that events—including a worldwide inflation, large and fitful international capital flows, the lack of a dominant currency such as the United States dollar formerly had been, and the sudden increase in oil prices with a consequent distortion of the whole international balance-of-payments network—had overtaken its deliberations. It decided that reform of the international monetary system in the existing situation would have to be a matter of evolution under political as well as technical economic guidance.

Having made this decision the Committee of Twenty folded up its papers, presented its recommendations for immediate action on certain subsidiary matters to the Executive Directors of the IMF, and adopted a final report containing an outline of longer term principles of international monetary behavior to be submitted to the Board of Governors of the IMF at its annual meeting in September 1974. The Committee of Twenty then ceased to exist.

The various actions or recommendations of the Committee subsequently adopted, or approved for further consideration, by the appropriate bodies of the IMF are too numerous and detailed to recount here, nor is it necessary to recite them all in order to appreciate the difficulties which a technical committee, such as the Committee of Twenty, found it impossible to surmount. They had to be passed on for ministerial consideration by finance ministers and such, who could take account of the political as well as the economic aspects of this whole exercise in political economy.

Two or three of the proposals for immediate action can be mentioned, however, to carry the story forward. They are:

(1) That an Interim Committee of the Board of Governors of the IMF, made up of ministerial members of the Board, should be established to advise the Board with regard to the management and adaptation of the international monetary system through the present troubled times, and until a permanent and representative Council of Governors with decision-making powers can be brought into being by amendment of the Articles of Agreement of the Fund. This would be, in essence, an executive committee of the Board of Governors which would meet several times a year between the annual meetings of the full board. A necessary administrative improvement.

(2) That guidelines be set forth for the management of floating exchange rates since the Fund, under the present articles of agreement, cannot legally promulgate and enforce rules for this purpose. The guidelines, which were later approved by the IMF, are based on the assumption that in a situation of floating exchange rates it may be desirable (a) to smooth out very short fluctuations in market rates, (b) to offer a measure of resistance to market tendencies in the slightly longer run when they are leading to unduly rapid movements in the rate, and (c) to the extent possible to form a reasonable estimate of the medium-term norm for a country's exchange rate, and to resist movements in market rates that appear to be deviating substantially from that norm. But the guidelines also take into account that national policies, including those relating to domestic stabilization, should not be subjected to greater constraints than are clearly necessary in the international interest. And if that sounds like a lawyer or an economist or a spokesman following a Summit Conference kicking up a lot of dust to obscure a lack of content, it is.

(3) That the method of establishing the value of special drawing rights which can be created by the IMF (in order to increase international liquidity in much the same way that national governments or central banks create domestic reserves) be changed from a direct link with the United States dollar and, through it with gold, to a link with a basket of currencies of sixteen countries that have a substantial share in the world's export of goods and services. This change, which has been made, resulted in a partial divorce of special drawing rights, an international reserve unit, from the United States dollar which had become an unsteady reference point.

The Board of Governors of the IMF at its meeting in September 1974, formally established the Interim Committee of Governors, recommended by the Committee of Twenty, to pick up where the Twenty left off. For the rest, the Board took note of the finding of the Committee of Twenty that it will be some time before a reformed international monetary system can be agreed upon and established, and endorsed the Committee's proposal that, in the interim, the Fund and its member states should pursue the general objectives and observe the general principles outlined by the Committee.

These objectives and principles envisage a reformed international monetary system which will include:

(1) An effective and symmetrical adjustment process, including a better functioning of the exchange rate regime based on stable but adjustable par values, but with floating rates recognized as providing a useful technique in particular situations. A neat straddle of a sticky point;

(2) Cooperation in dealing with disequilibrating capital flows. A pious hope;

(3) The introduction of an appropriate form of convertibility for the settlement of imbalances among the countries of the world, which means allowing as much freedom as possible for individual countries to choose the composition of their reserves, whether gold, special drawing rights, or reserve currencies such as the United States dollar;

(4) An obligation laid upon all countries, both those in surplus and those in deficit in their payments balances, to assure effective and timely payments adjustments. Another pious hope;

(5) Better international management of global liquidity, with special drawing rights becoming the principal reserve asset, the role of gold and reserve currencies being reduced, and the official price of gold being abolished. A tough nut still uncracked.

In terms of the bright hopes or, perhaps, the enforced show of confidence in finding early solutions of difficult problems, when official reform of the international monetary system was first undertaken in 1972, this catalogue of frustration might be said to be where we came in. That, of course, would not be wholly fair. The ground work for a second phase of discussion and negotiation at the ministerial or politico-economic level has been put in place by the technical committee, and some of the underbrush surrounding the more important issues has been cleared out. Nevertheless, the difficulties in the way of reaching acceptable solutions, or compromises, of the hard-core major problems which are at the center of our international monetary difficulties cannot be minimized. Too many vital concerns of individual nations and groups of nations are involved, motives of self-interest and self-protection are strong, and the leadership of the more powerful nations in promoting international cooperation is at a low ebb.

To summarize: The most intractable issues which still will face the annual meeting of the Board of Governors of the International Monetary Fund in Washington next month are:

(1) Finding an international adjustment process with respect to balances of payments of individual countries, and gaining acceptance of the joint responsibility of all countries for the correction of imbalances, both countries whose payments are in surplus and countries whose payments are in deficit, while preserving the independence of each nation to conduct its domestic economic affairs without international constraint.

(2) Deciding the question of whether stable but adjustable par values or floating rates for national currencies are to be the system norm. The hopes that floating rates would provide an automatic or market solution of the adjustment problem have not been realized in practice. Their apparent success in avoiding periodic monetary crises during the past two years has derived more from an overlay of continuing all-embracing crisis rather than from their inherent contribution to stability.

(3) Managing the problem of international liquidity, including the volume of such liquidity and its composition as between gold, special drawing rights, and national currency reserves, which includes the immediate problem of shrinking the tremendous increase in international reserves during the recent years which contributed to a worldwide inflation.

Essentially these are the same problems which brought down the Bretton Woods Agreements and which the International Monetary Fund set out to correct in 1972. A bicycle theory of monetary reform appears to have emerged from these deliberations. We have avoided falling flat, but the emphasis so far has been on staying erect; the bicycle hasn't really been going anywhere.

This may be the correct posture in the present disordered state of world economic affairs, and it appears to be the posture which has been publicly assumed by our government. Nevertheless I would like to see the bicycle discreetly developing some forward motion, and I think the United States, West Germany, and Japan (with possibly the United Kingdom and France) should now take the lead in bringing this about. These three (or five) nations have the financial, trading, and industrial muscle and the developed financial markets necessary to form the core of any new or reformed international monetary system. Their approach at this stage could be low-key, as was the case before Bretton Woods when competent senior officials of the United States and the United Kingdom were quietly and more or less informally assigned the task of developing plans which later were placed before the wider world community for consideration. I do not think it wise or prudent to rely wholly on evolution to do the job for us.

Excerpts from the remarks of Allan Sproul at the Board of Directors Meetings, Wells Fargo Bank, San Francisco, California, August 16, 1977

Beneath the welter of economic statistics which are published almost weekly, reflecting various developments in the national and international business and credit situations with varying degrees of accuracy, at least two major problems have thus far defied the solvents of market forces and the ministrations of governments.

On the domestic front we are still groping to find a way between the dangers of inflation and the dangers of unemployment. These two economic scourges, which in earlier and simpler times were supposed to be antithetical, have now been in cohabitation for several years, and we have yet to find a remedy for their behavior, a remedy which is socially, politically, and economically acceptable. Both the rate of inflation and the rate of unemployment in the United States remain at historically high and disturbing levels.

Internationally, we do not have a monetary system which will respond quickly and adequately to the inevitable ups and downs of international trade and capital movements, while maintaining a degree of exchange stability which is necessary for the most effective accommodation of world trade, and the making of sound commitments in real terms to move financial capital or to make direct investments outside one's own country. Floating exchange rates have not proved to be a panacea in a world of nation states in which wide disparities of national economic performance exist and persist. . . .

The utopian international monetary system would consist of a single world money, and a world central bank which would provide the necessary liquidity to accommodate the growth of world trade, and would act as a lender of last resort in the case of individual countries facing temporarily severe but not necessarily fatal economic strains. The infringements of national sovereignty which such a system might involve, and the interference with national economic and social programs with which its requirements might conflict, provide assurance that the emergence of such a system is impossible in the present world of nation states.

We have always had to get along with much less. In the nineteenth century the British were the dominant factor in world trade and finance, and the Bank of England more or less managed the so-called gold and gold exchange standards of international monetary intercourse. This system disappeared between the two world wars, with the decline of British influence and power in world trade and finance. In the immediate post-World War II period, the United States and the United States dollar partially assumed the privileges and burdens of this hegemony, but the United States tired of the role when it was deemed to be working against our national interests in the early 1970s and shucked it.

The nearest thing we now have to an international arbiter—an institutional apparatus which can try to balance the scales between national policies of price stability and maximum employment, and the international need for competitive trade expansion, reasonably stable exchanges, and interlocking credit and capital markets (including the Eurocurrency and bond markets)—is the International Monetary Fund. But that organization, somewhat like the United Nations, is beset by an organizational structure which, in deference to the power of the great industrial countries and the "democratic" demands of the less powerful, less developed countries, is enmeshed in a variety of veto provisions which practically deprive it of the attributes needed for its major tasks. Veto power on important actions has been given to the United States, to the European Economic Community, to the Organization of the Petroleum Exporting Countries, and to the "Committee of 77" which now numbers about 140 lesser countries. This is a recipe for diffusion of authority and responsibility which is almost fatal.

What we are left with, in terms of an international monetary system, are periodic meetings of the finance ministers of the principal countries, and periodic statements of intent to keep their countries in phase so far as economic growth and price stability are concerned, and to keep the values of their currencies in some sort of equilibrium.

Such international good intentions falter, however, in the face of disparate economic performances of the various countries, widening foreign trade and current account deficits and surpluses, and substantial fluctuations in currency values. There follows debate as to who should take action to defend the shaky structure, *i.e.*, should it be West Germany and Japan and other countries with large trade surpluses and strong currencies or should it be the United States and other countries with large trade deficits and relatively weaker currencies. Meanwhile nontariff import and export restrictions for protectionist purposes proliferate, leading to losses in international efficiency and economic well-being. This is economic retrogression on a world basis.

My own opinion is that, eventually, the international monetary system will have to move back toward a regime of fixed rates, or strongly managed rates which approximate fixed rates, in a world which apart from the communist states is more and more becoming one large international economic entity. In such a development the United States, as the largest trading nation and the largest capital market, should play a leading part, and the United States dollar which is still the principal transactions currency of the world and the principal reserve currency of much of the world should have a leading role. "Benign neglect" of the exchange value of the dollar, which the United States Treasury still seems to espouse from time to time, is not a tenable policy.

Remarks of Allan Sproul at the Board of Directors Meeting, Wells Fargo Bank, San Francisco, California, November 15, 1977

The domestic economy is in partial disarray, a situation which is disturbing but not fatal. It is in disarray politically and it is in disarray economically, reminding us that our field of concern is political economy, not just economics in a textbook sense.

Politically, too many difficult and contentious problems have been heaped by the President on a Congress conditioned by years of feuding with the executive branch of government. This has meant that the first nine months of our first administration in eight years, in which the two branches of government have been controlled by the same political party, have been spent more largely in Byzantine maneuvering of Congressional committees than in bringing to passage important measures dealing with urgent economic problems. The energy problem, and the tax changes needed to put new life into the ongoing recovery from the 1974-75 recession, have been left dangling.

Harried by a mixture of contending political and economic forces, and with the persistent problems of unemployment and inflation still inflicting social and economic costs on business and consumers, the underlying strength of the domestic economy is overlaid with a fog of uncertainty. And that is where I am going to leave it, in the hope that during the next few months the fog will lift and the future will become less obscure.

Meanwhile our international economic position is plagued with its own uncertainties. It is misleading, of course, to separate sharply our foreign and our domestic affairs. They intermingle with and react on one another in a multitude of ways. But, for purposes of examination, it is possible to focus on certain international aspects of our trading and financial situation so that we can look more closely at matters which recently have forced themselves on our attention. I am referring to the large deficit in our trading accounts with the rest of the world and to the signs of incipient weakness of the dollar in the foreign exchange markets.

Balance-of-payments statistics are tricky. The various components of the total balance react on one another in a variety of ways at different times and in different circumstances, and detailed interpretation of the figures is an arcane accomplishment of specialists, which I am not. Even the conception itself—a double-entry system of international bookkeeping, in which assets and liabilities must balance—has its weaknesses as a reflection of the real world. Nevertheless the figures do offer guides to opinion and to policy.

The main emphasis, recently, has been on the development of a massive deficit in our balance of trade during the past nine months, which it is now estimated will be $25 billion or more during the calendar year. A more significant figure, perhaps, is our balance of payments on current account which, in addition to trade, includes net revenues on services, military transactions, and investment income from abroad. Together, a favorable balance on these latter items may offset about half our deficit on trade, but the deficit thus reduced will still be of record and disturbing proportions.

The figure needed to offset the remaining half of the trade deficit—that is to balance the books—is an inflow of foreign capital, including some long-term funds, but probably consisting to a large extent of short-term funds seeking employment in our broad financial markets, while serving as transaction balances and reserves of the countries of origin and their nationals. This is in part, of course, our contribution to the process of recycling the petrodollars continuing to pile up on the books of the OPEC countries. The OPEC surplus with the rest of the world is estimated at $37 billion this year, and is expected to continue at about this annual rate for sometime ahead. For our markets to help recycle some of these funds is constructive, but to become too largely involved in the process is dangerous.

This imbalance is the monetary face of the energy crisis and is at the core of our balance-of-payments problem. It bears seed which could sprout into serious international monetary instability. At worst, it could degenerate into persistent weakness of the dollar, creating the kind of monetary crisis which developed in the late 1960s when other nations (and their nationals and some of our nationals) developed a growing reluctance to add to or even maintain their dollar holdings. On that occasion the movement finally led to the complete breakdown of the existing international monetary arrangements.

Floating or freely flexible exchange rates, according to their more fervent advocates, were supposed to correct such maladjustments in the future by bringing about equilibrating movements of trade and capital between nations. They were to be the lubricant of the international adjustment process. But the exchange rate flexibility of the past four years does not seem to have played much of a role in reducing external imbalances. These imbalances have been dominated by other factors.

This is not surprising. The difficulties of the international adjustment process have always been at the center of weakness of international monetary arrangements. Politically and economically such adjustments collide with domestic realities. They impinge upon national rates of economic growth, of inflation, of employment and unemployment; they impinge on the survival of critical national export and import interests; and they foster trade and speculative responses to disparate national monetary and fiscal policies. National governments have been unable or unwilling, or both, to surrender their prerogatives in these matters wholly to the foreign exchange markets.

Summit meetings and meetings of finance ministers from Rangoon to Rambouillet, and pronouncements of the IMF, have exhorted the nations to coordinate their domestic economic policies with their international economic responsibilities. The overall result has been a surplus of communiqués and not much concrete action.

Now, in its own defense, the United States should take the lead in seeking a contribution to a solution of this general problem. It will have to bring about a major improvement in its own international position, and in the strength of the dollar which is still the center of the world's monetary machinery. It will have to quit dragging its feet and get on with the business of adopting an effective energy policy.

The need for such a policy has existed for four long years, at least, since the Arab oil embargo and the subsequent increase in OPEC oil prices from $2.53 to $13.25 a barrel in 1973, and nothing equal to the task has been accomplished. United States net imports of fuels during 1977 have been running at an annual rate of about $40 billion, and this is by far the biggest cause of our overall trade deficit. Our record of response to the problem has been the worst of the principal industrial countries. Since 1973, oil consumption in the United States has increased substantially while consumption in other principal industrial countries such as the United Kingdom, Germany, France, Italy, and Japan has decreased by effective amounts in terms of need.

To get some real mileage in reversing present trends in our balance of payments, and in preventing further weakness of the dollar, further disturbances in the international monetary system, and further slippage of the world into restrictive trade practices, we shall have to move quickly and decisively to adopt an energy policy which will begin the process of curtailing the enormous volume and value of our oil and gas imports. There are grave domestic questions involved in existing energy proposals. But so far as the balance of payments is concerned the evidence is unambiguous and clear. The bargains and compromises must be struck. Time is running out.